A Bunch of Rosés

Phillip Humphries

Illustrated by Tamsin Hazelwood

ISBN: 978-1-291-72077-8

Edition: First Edition January 2014

Copyright: © 2014 Phillip Humphries

License: Standard copyright license

Printed: Lulu Publishing

All rights reserved.

Contents

Introduction	4
How It's Made	6
Wine and you	10
A Potted History	12
Styles of Wine	15
Wines and Grapes	71
Rosé in (just over) a Page - The Do's And Don'ts	76
The Price of Wine	78
Some Views from the Experts	81
Sources	85

Introduction

This book is all about Rosé wine, just in case you were misled by the title. My aim is to share with you all my enthusiasm for this delightful drink and in the process convince you that it is "proper" wine.

As you browse through you will find all manner of information about the making, growing, marketing and above all drinking of rosé around the world. What you will not find is one of those shopping lists of wines that you have never heard of and cannot find which goes out of date faster than a newspaper. I will slip in the odd interesting bottle but the aim is that you should come out the other side knowing a bit more about wine and have some tips about identifying something you will enjoy, and in the end of the day wine is not about study and science it is about enjoyment.

For many it seems rosé is seen at best as a bit of a lightweight sideshow and at worst as something of a joke being played on people who are being conned into believing this is actually wine and not some sort of posh alco-pop! Given you are reading this far I am guessing you may have a wine book or two in the shelf? Check it out – how much space is devoted to Rosé wine? It may get a sidebar or a footnote but really very little is said about it. Rosé is in reality a wine of countless guises, made from a plethora of grape varieties, in a range of styles which suit it to any occasion. In fact there are appellations in France which *only* make rosé wines.

In 2008 the French bought more rosé than white wine, and that trend has continued. Worldwide 25.3 million hectoliters of rosé wine were produced in 2010, a 13% increase in production over the previous 8 years. This means that rosé now accounts for 10% of worldwide wine production. This is no mere sideshow it is a big event, one to which you should buy a ticket and bring a picnic – quite literally!

So, come with me as we don our rosé coloured glasses and discover the world of rosé wines....

How It's Made

Rosé wine uses techniques from both red and white wine making to produce a wine which has characteristics of both. In some cases the red character may be held to a minor role of just providing the colour but at the other end of the spectrum it brings structure, flavour and even tannin to the glass.

Now when asked how to make rosé wine how many people do you think will say "mix red and white wine"? In my experience as close to 100% as makes no difference. Well, for the most part this is not actually what is done. However, surprisingly enough this is an approved legitimate method for making rosé champagne, but more of this later. Anyway let's get down to business. Just how does rosé get made? Let us put ourselves in the position of a winemaker whose primary objective is to make a rosé wine. The usual method will be to start our as if we were making a red wine. You can make white wine from black or white grapes because the inside is the more or less same colour irrespective of the skin. Black grapes encompasses all the red, purple black coloured grapes and white is all the green ones right through to the very slightly pinkish looking grapes which go into Gewürztraminer. However, to make red wine you have to start with black grapes because all that colour comes from the skins.

So, we are going to select some black grapes for making our wine. The grapes once picked may be sorted to ensure only the best bunches go on to make wine - we may as well start this journey thinking about a really good bottle of wine. Since we are making good wine let's de-stem the bunches, this means removing the grapes from the stem they grow on, because these can add some extra bitterness and tannin which we don't want in our wine.

The de-stemming process will crush the grapes breaking their skins and allowing the juice to flow out. Now we macerate - that just means letting the skins sit in the juice for a short while. we do this because Now if we were making red wine this might be several days, indeed we would probably go on to ferment the wine with the skins still in there.

After 12 to 24 hours, in some cases even less, we are going to drain off the juice which will by now have taken on as much colour as we need. This grape juice is now going to be fermented as if we were making a white wine. This means fermenting it at 16 to 20 degrees, cooler than for a red wine, which will preserve the fruitiness of the wine.

So our next job is to transfer the juice in to a stainless steel fermentation vessel where we can exercise careful control over the temperature, and of course ensure absolute hygiene which is needed at all stages of wine making if we are not to produce very expensive vinegar.

Sometimes winemakers will allow malolactic fermentation to take place when making white wines. This bacterial fermentation converts malic acid in the wine to lactic acid, the acidity you find in milk, which can give wine a more rounded creaminess. As we are making a wine which is going to be fruity and refreshing we will put a stop to that by chilling the wine once the alcoholic fermentation reaches the point we want.

Now about that alcoholic fermentation. If we wanted a dry wine we would let that continue until all the sugar which was in the grapes has been used up and turned in to alcohol. However, we can also choose to stop the fermentation earlier which will leave a bit of sweetness in the wine. I think today we are going to go for fermentation to dryness. Now if we were making a red or white wine we might be thinking about ageing this wine in oak barrels at this point but this is a rosé so let's get it in a bottle. That's it we have a bottle of rosé wine which is ready to drink right now.

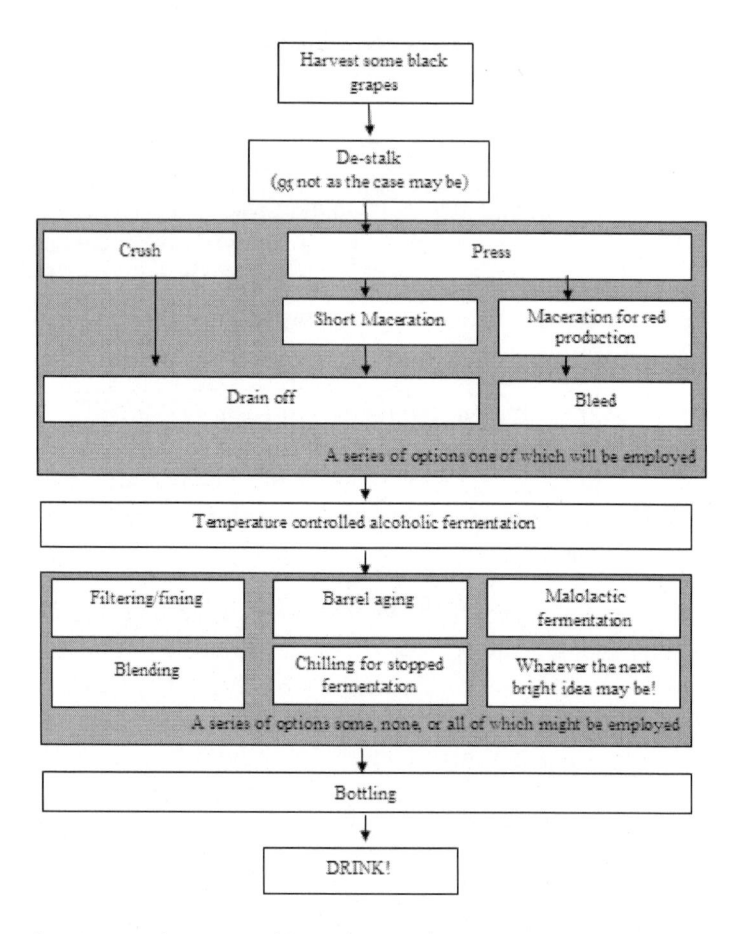

```
         Harvest some black
              grapes
                │
                ▼
           De-stalk
      (or not as the case may be)
                │
                ▼
┌─────────────────────────────────────────────┐
│  Crush              Press                    │
│    │                  │                      │
│    │                  ▼                      │
│    │         Short Maceration    Maceration for red
│    │                                production │
│    ▼                  ▼                  ▼   │
│         Drain off              Bleed         │
│                                              │
│   A series of options one of which will be employed │
└─────────────────────────────────────────────┘
                │
                ▼
    Temperature controlled alcoholic fermentation
                │
                ▼
┌─────────────────────────────────────────────┐
│ Filtering/fining   Barrel aging   Malolactic │
│                                   fermentation│
│                                              │
│  Blending      Chilling for stopped  Whatever the next│
│                  fermentation        bright idea may be!│
│                                              │
│ A series of options some, none, or all of which might be employed │
└─────────────────────────────────────────────┘
                │
                ▼
            Bottling
                │
                ▼
             DRINK!
```

So, that is your basic Rosé but as I have said there are a whole range of styles that rosé can appear in so the winemaking process can vary widely. The process above is not a set of rules, it is just a basic tune upon which the individual winemaker can play any number of variations like a jazz musician.

One classic variation is called "Vin Gris". Now although this is French for grey wine, which sounds very unappetising, it actually denotes a very pale pink wine which is made by the process we just went through but without any maceration. So, the grapes are crushed and pressed and the juice goes straight on to fermentation.

This process uses lightly coloured grapes such as Cinsault, Gamay and Grenache Gris.

Another of the principal variations has led to what might be termed "the war of the rosés "- well it might be if you had no shame about bad puns like me. This is the Saingnée method – literally bleeding the juice from red wine making very early in the process before it has taken on too much colour. In fact this process is being used to increase the colour of the red wine because all the skins stay behind but in less juice as some has been drawn off thereby making the remainder more concentrated. In Bordeaux it used to be that this drained off wine would quite literally be that - sent down the drain! But economics being what they are many winemakers realised there could be a double benefit – a concentrated red wine and the makings of a rosé. So what's the problem? Well François Millo, president of the Provence Wine Council (CIVP) has slammed saignée method rosé as "not true rosé." In May 2012 at the London International Wine Fair he said people who make saignée rosé are opportunists. In their mind they are making red wine – the rosé just happens to be a by-product. The saignée method is a bad way of making rosé. The wine is more of an afterthought; very few people in Provence use it. 85% of the wine we produce in Provence is rosé, so it's at the top of our priority list – our grapes are grown for rosé and our harvest is done for rosé,"

Now Provence is home to some of the best rosé wines so you can understand he may want to "big up" his own producers but the technique has its supporters too. For example Francis Boulard makes a rosé champagne called "Rosé de Saignée" which is made by just this method, so it can't be that much of a sin! Elsewhere the likes of Sébastien Gavillet, an international wine judge, declare that " Saigneé or bleeding is used to make the best quality rosé wines".

Wine and you

Wine is a complicated concoction. Although 80 to 90% is just water there are around 1000 other components including alcohol, sugar, acids, minerals, vitamins and trace elements. In particular there are also a class of compounds called polyphenols which includes tannins, flavonoids and anthocyanins, which are largely responsible for the colour in red, and of course rosé, wines.

Louis Pasteur declared wine to be "...the most healthful and most hygienic of beverages". Indeed the French have a fine tradition of regarding wine essentially as a health food. In 1990 it was Health magazine that set out the paradox that whilst the French diet was very rich they experienced relatively low levels of heart disease. The American Cardiologist Arthur Klatsky found that those who had 2-3 glasses of tannic red wine a day had lower levels of cardiac issues than those who drank no wine at all

How about that curse of modern society, the fad diet? Well, wine can contribute to weight loss as part of a calorie controlled diet. Of course Foie Gras and clotted cream can contribute to weight loss part of a calorie controlled diet! It all depends on how you decide to distribute your allocated calories - one well-buttered cheese toastie or spread them out with some sensible food through the course of the day. Wine though is not the enemy of the slimmer. A small (10cl), ok so make that very small, glass of 12% abv red wine contains just shy of 90kCals, but the same glass of rosé has only 87kCals. If you really are inspired by wine as a route to weight loss your best bet is champagne at a mere 81kCals.

There is even a wine based Spa for treating all your ills based at Chateau Smith-Haut-Lafitte. The Spa de Vinotherapie Caudalie offers red wine baths, a Sauvignon massage and honey and wine body wraps. This is all based on those polyphenols mentioned earlier which have antioxidant properties which by neutralising the free radicals (possibly also a partisan group set up in the late fifties?) can offset the effects of aging. Indeed they produce arrange of cosmetics based on red grape skins which are said to improve the elasticity of the skin. Of course you could just quaff a bottle and worry a bit less about the wrinkles. So popular has this been that they now have vinotherapie spas in three French cities as well as New York and Bilbao.

Of course men and women think differently about aging and they also think differently about wine. By and large women tend to like *vins flateurs,* more subtle aromatic wines with a pronounced bouquet and very smooth tannins. Men on the other hand like something , well, more macho with a powerful palate and punchy tannins. Perhaps this is why some, as yet unenlightened commentators, see wine only as a ladies drink? Having let it be known I was writing this book I got a few interesting comments over the LinkedIn group I frequent - one of which was that rosé wine is "...wine with training wheels", although this comment did come from an American so they had probably only ever experienced blush wines which whilst very pleasant I can sort of see where he was coming from.

A Potted History

Wine it is thought has been on the menu for around 7000 years. Imagine the scene, grapes were collected as a sweet treat in the diet and perhaps stored in jars. In order to spread the treat over as long a period as possible they were kept that little bit too long. After a while they start to go squishy (technical term!) Now then, grapes have a very light powdery bloom on the outside which is actually wild yeast. So what do you know we are starting to make wine! Some brave soul would have been the first to taste this concoction and presumably pronounced it "Good!"

More recently in 2004 the tale of wine was pushed back as far as the stone age when Patrick McGovern through combining chemical analysis and archaeology was able to show that traces of wine go back to the Neolithic period some 8,500BC. The search for the first domesticated grapevines is focussed on Eastern Turkey where many domesticated crops came from.

It is likely that these first deliberate wines were in fact rosé wines. Mixes of grapes gathered and crushed to release the juice and then skins quickly discarded leaving the juice with just a little colour. The Egyptians had a neat trick of crushing the grapes in a large cloth which was then twisted as you might wring out a dishcloth to squeeze out as much juice as possible. It is thought that the first wine was produced in Georgia where it was fermented in pots buried in the ground – very useful for moderating the temperature of the fermentation, and presumably hiding it from any local n'ere do wells.

Over time as you might expect through a little ingenuity we got better at producing wine that we enjoyed. One of the key discoveries in this process was that grapes from the Vitis Vinifera vine make really good wine and it is this species of vine that the vast majority of wine is now made from. Likewise we moved away from the pot luck of wild yeasts to using cultivated yeast, mainly *Saccharomyces cerevisiae*, as the fermentation agent.

In the world of rosé Provence in the south of France has staked its claim to be the spiritual home of the pink drink. The Greeks founded a colony in what is now Marseille some 2,600 years ago and being a sophisticated people who knew how to prioritise they immediately set to planting vines and making wine, rosé wine. This information is provided, entirely independently, by the council Interprofessional de Vins de Provence (CIVP)!

Although Bordeaux is now known best for powerful red wines its reputation was founded in the seventeen the century on a wine called Clairet. Sound familiar? Yes, that is where we get the word Claret from, and our devotion to Bordeaux wines, not to mention an incentive to go to war to hang onto that bit of France for ourselves. The best original Bordeaux wines were known as vins d'une nuit or wines of one night as they sat on the skins for only a single night. Clairet therefore was a much lighter wine that those Bordeaux produces today, indeed it could (and I will) be described as a rosé. So all you folk with your "en primeur" Bordeaux wines just think on where the heritage of that comes from.

They did make wines of a deeper red by allowing a longer maceration but these were harsh rough wines and seen as much lower quality, although had they kept them for a few yours who knows how good they might have been? Enough romance – they would have been horrible because the conditions were hardly antiseptic and bacteria love a nice drop of wine as much as the rest of us so it would like as not have turned to vinegar.

Entirely by the way let me mention that in researching the history of wine I visited the Donjon de Sigournais near Chantonnay as they pitched one of their main attractions as an Exposition "Le vin et la vigne au moyen age" - wine and vines in the middle ages - so you can see the attraction. Well, this turns out to be three small posters in a side room, one saying wine has a history, one saying monks made a lot of wine and one extolling the dubious virtues of a rather boring white grape the Folle Blanche (thin acidic white wine with a low alcohol level). If you are ever passing that way my advice is to keep going!

Styles of Wine

Rosé has a guise for all occasions. Celebration – it has to be champagne. Rosé champagne has all that opulence you would expect but also brings a spirit of fun. I would go for a Brut which is just off dry with the sophistication of true champagne flavours but with a hint of strawberry and summer about it. Serve well chilled

Party time – Let's go for a sparkling rosé. Champagne due to the process of production is always going to be relatively expensive but that's no reason to forego a bit of sparkle.

Picnic – Here we want something light and quaffable which is not going to have us under the table, or under the rug (actually that does not sound such a bad idea! Sorry, must try to behave) so how about something with some sweetness and low alcohol. A blush Zinfandel is just the thing – strawberries and cream in a glass. The garden party – I think here we want a little more sophistication but still something light with a little sweetness so perhaps an Anjou Rosé.

The dinner party – People seldom think of rosé with food but a dry rosé made from classic black grapes such as Cabernet Sauvignon or Syrah can easily deliver the flavour and structure you need to complement food. You will even detect some tannin in these wines so we can start pairing them with something more sturdy than chicken – perhaps veal or gammon.

Drinking with Friends – Rosé is a sociable drink, although people are snobbish about it given a warm summer afternoon, a few friends, a dish of olives, almost everyone will welcome a glass of dry rosé. As this is the classic occasion let's have a classic wine from Tavel in the southern Rhone.

Rosé Around the World

Generally speaking as we move south (in the northern hemisphere) it is going to get warmer and as we move inland summers will be hotter and winters colder. This variation in climate plays a large part in determining not only what grapes will grow but also how they will grow. Too little sun and they will not ripen, the sugar will not build up and the flavours will be sour and grassy. Too much sun and the grape will build up lots of sugar but have little acidity. Too much rain the flavours will be diluted. The same happens if a vineyard is over worked to produce yields the ground just does not have the capabilities of sustaining.

The game the winemaker has to play with rosé as with any other wine is to balance acidity, alcohol, sweetness, flavour, and yield to produce wine economically in the style he wants. There are various

---

Phylloxera

This is actually a tiny beetle which chews in to the roots which then get infected and it is this infection which kills off the vine. American rootstock once bitten exudes a sap which seals up the hole – like a self-repairing tyre. Isn't it brilliant the Americans can bail us out like this? Well, er, it was the Americans who gave us Phylloxera in the first place! The reason they have resistant roots is that their vines have had it for so long they have evolved this defense mechanism.

---

tricks he has up his sleeve to help him overcome these difficulties. Careful site selection is the first thing, after all if you get this wrong uprooting the vineyard to move it 100m to the left would be pretty annoying! The site needs to provide both the right soil and also the right aspect. Vines generally like a free draining soil they can really push their roots down into. There need to be enough nutrients but over-abundance can cause as many problems as scarcity. If we are in a cool climate it can be good to have quite stony ground to reflect the sunlight up in to the vines during the day and act as a sort of storage radiator overnight.

The aspect and location of the site needs to find that place in the landscape where the vines are protected from winds and enjoy as much sunlight as possible. It is also important to think about where fog and frost pockets may form. These can be useful for some wines but not for rosé.

OK, having got ourselves a site we need to plant some vines. For the most part vines come with the variety of choice, say cabernet sauvignon, grafted onto an American vine rootstock. This is because there is a pest called phylloxera which since the nineteenth century has been making a meal of vines around the world and killing them off. The American roots are resistant to this so unless you are working somewhere this little beast has not colonised that is what you use. Now the vine is in and growing we need to train it. This does not entail a whip and a chair (although no doubt there is someone in California prepared to give this a go). This means pruning and supporting the vine to make the best use of the site. So if you are likely to have misty mornings like the vineyards across England you will tend to train the vines higher to keep them out of the worst of this. If you have steep slopes and high winds like in the Northern Rhone each vine may get a stay of its own.

As the vine grows the aim is to keep it healthy and on schedule so come harvest the grapes have reached the right level of maturity. This means pruning the leaves to ensure there are enough to ensure photosynthesis but not too many that the grapes are shaded from the sun, unless you are in a particularly hot climate in which case you desperately need to shade the grapes to avoid sunburn (yes really). As the grapes grow those producers aiming for very high quality wine will judiciously cut off some early bunches to ensure that those that are left get all the vine's attention – this is known in the trade as the "Green Harvest" as at this stage black grapes have not yet started to take on any colour so are green.

Assuming all of this goes well and the crop is not destroyed by an autumnal hail storm we arrive at harvest time, in France the vendange. There are still teams of people with big baskets who tramp though the vineyards gathering in the grapes by hand but this is usually where the producer is making a high quality wine and wishes to exclude the unripe or rotten grapes or else the site is too steep or narrow to allow for mechanical harvesting. Other times this would happen are in the production of particular wines where you want to select grapes affected by "noble rot" from which are made exceptional, lusciously sweet wines. There is another circumstance which is where labour prices are simply so cheap or the producer so poor that machine harvesting does not make financial sense. Later on I will mount the hobbyhorse of wine prices!

France

As already cited the French drink an enormous amount of rosé wine, more even than white wine, so it is fitting that we start our journey in France. In fact France produced more than 6.5 million hectolitres of rosé wine in 2010, making it the world leader with 26% of total production.

So let us start our journey here. No doubt to the chagrin of the CIVP we will travel from North to South.

The Loire Valley

The Loire region is the home of one of the most famous rosé wines, Rosé d'Anjou. The Loire runs roughly 1012Km from the Cévennes in the Ardèche to run in to the sea at St Nazaire. Inland the climate is a cool continental but as we get toward the sea progressively becomes more maritime, so more like the English climate – cool and wet!

Anjou comes from the area around Blois which is about halfway down the Loire. Here there are two appellations – Rosé d'Anjou and Cabernet d'Anjou.

The first of these is the most well-known and is made from a grape called Grolleau, sometimes called Groslot. The rules of the AOC permit Gamay and Malbec varieties to be used in blending the wine but in practice very little is ever used. This is particular to this region and is not used anywhere else. It is a high yielding grape which is just as well given the demand for the wine. Anjou Rosé is a light wine as most rosés are but it has that little bit of sweetness which makes it very appealing as a drink for those lazy summer afternoons.

A lunchtime Rosé d'Anjou in Nantes

Now if that all sounds a bit frivolous you may be more tempted by Cabernet d'Anjou. This is an off dry wine made from Cabernet Sauvignon and Cabernet Franc. These are grapes well known for their use in red wine; Cabernet Sauvignon in particular is the king of the left bank in Bordeaux making all those really expensive wines from Haut Brion and Margaux. The thing is it only just manages to ripen in Bordeaux which is why they have the insurance policy of a lot of Merlot vines which ripen earlier and easier. Angers is further north so we are really pushing it here if we expect this grape to ripen. Being a rosé the wine does not have that high level of tannin extraction which might be a problem but as the grapes have really struggled to ripen there is a high level of acidity in the wine. I know this sounds pretty unappetising but it is the acidity in wine that makes it refreshing and balances the other components so I am not saying "here have a glass of battery acid". In fact the acidity in this wine makes it one of the few rosé wines which can age well. So after all that the cabernet sauvignon is still doing its job just like in Bordeaux.

Stretching across a large part of the Loire valley is another wine designation which is for Rosé de Loire, this is again an AOC wine but the rules are a little looser. This can be made from grapes gathered from vineyards across 5 Départements through the Loire valley. It uses Cabernet grapes which must account for at least 30% of the blend with Grolleau, Pineau d'Aunis, Pinot Noir and Gamay. These grapes therefore are grown on a wide variety of soils from the Tuffeau of Saumur to the Schistes of Anjou. Below this lies the IGP designation of Val de Loire. You either see this as something which releases the true creativity of the winemaker or a licence to make wine the cheapest way possible depending on whether you have had a nice one or not. One I would especially recommend from the area is the AOC Valencay Rosé from Hubert et Olivier Sinson right out at the extreme edge of the Touraine AOC area near Meusnes. Here they use Gamay, Pinot Noir, and Malbec, or Cot as it is known locally, to make a dry wine with a light tannin structure and aromas of crushed nettles and a palate of red fruits with a little earthiness.

A lovely story I came across is that of Christine & Joel Ménard who own and operate Domaine des Sablonnettes near Rablay Sur Layon in the Loire. They produce a delightful light wine from Cabernet Franc and Cabernet Sauvignon which is just that bit too red to be called a rosé according to the powers that be. They still manage to get Rosé proudly onto the label though by taking an idea from René Magritte and call the wine "Anjou Ceci n'est pas un rosé". It is described as being a little like a Beaujolais Fleurie with red fruits and some well balanced earthiness.

Further on downstream the Loire passes Chinon. This is the home of the Cabernet Franc. Normally found blended with its more up market cousins Merlot and Cabernet Sauvignon here they show of what they can do with the grape on its own. Naturally part of the show includes a rosé although you are going to have to be fairly diligent in your search to find it.

By the time we hit the sea the wine is all about crisp Muscadet ready for all that seafood. Although if we stretch things a bit further south in the Vendeé there is a much neglected wine area here producing some very drinkable wares which take advantage of the microclimate of the area which make it just that degree or two warmer than other sites along the coast. Here we have the AOC areas of Fiefs Vendéens, Marieul and Brem which produce white, red and naturally rosé wine. This is one of, if not the, newest awarded AOCs in France having attained this accolade only in 2011.

The rosé is made principally from Gamay and Pinot Noir generally with some Cabernet Franc thrown in for good measure. Here it is the classic production technique of maceration rather than the approach used in Beaujolais which we come to in a while. These are country wines and although the regions are recently elevated to AOC status many of the producers still make wine as Vin de France or Val de Loire wines often using wild yeast fermentations. This means that rather than adding a specific strain of yeast they are reliant on the natural yeast which appears as the faint bloom on the skins of the grapes.

Appellation

More often Appellation D'Origin Controlé (AOC) in the French system an appellation denotes a specific wine making area with a set of rules which govern many aspects of the wine production – grapes, yields, sugar content, alcohol content, shape of bottle! This is why some adventurous wine makers opt for the lower designation of Vin de Pays as this allows them far more freedom.

In the broader EU system this is the equivalent of Protected Designation of Origin (PDO).

Another EU wine designation you will see is Indication Géographique Protegé. More easily rendered IGP this is the rung below AOC wines. Wines with this designation judged to be characteristic of a particular region and are made in line with a set of agreed rules, albeit these are not as restrictive as AOC rules.

Now this is not a classic rose region but of course it is where they make Pink Champagne. This you will recall is the only pink wine in the EU which can legally be made by mixing red and white wines, although this is by no means compulsory still most rosé champagne is made by blending, although being as this is Champagne this process is called *assemblage* rather than mixing.

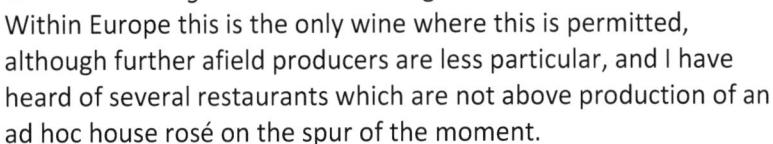

Within Europe this is the only wine where this is permitted, although further afield producers are less particular, and I have heard of several restaurants which are not above production of an ad hoc house rosé on the spur of the moment.

Producing sparkling wine by the traditional champagne method is a bit of an involved process. First you make a still wine, or for rosé champagne two still wines, a red and a white. If this really is champagne you have to work only with the permitted grape varieties Pinot Noir and Pinot Meunier for the black grapes and Chardonnay for the white grape. This initial wine is a dry wine and high in acidity.

The blend is then constructed from this new harvest wine and possibly some reserve wines which have been held back from previous years. In champagne (everything is special in champagne!) the appellation laws insist that producers retain a percentage of the harvest for blending.

Once we have mixed up a suitably pink still wine this is bottled in the famous thick champagne bottle. The bottles need to be thick because what we do next is dose it up with more yeast and some sugar to start a second fermentation, only this time we are going to keep all the carbon dioxide produced in the bottle which is secured with a crown cap – exactly like a bottle of beer.

This secondary fermentation will add more alcohol to the wine but also those toasty yeasty flavours that distinguish wines made by this method. After the fermentation process is finished and the wine has sat on the used up yeast, termed the lees, for a while to add more flavour and body to the wine then the process of getting the used up yeast out starts. In ye olden days this was done by hand by a man called a riddler (no not the arch enemy of Batman). Bottles would be loaded horizontally into a frame called a pulpitre and over a period of months the bottle would be turned and tilted very slowly until all the lees slid down the bottle and formed a deposit under the cap. Nowadays it is rather less romantic and bottles are loaded 500 at a time into a cage in a machine called a gyro palette, also in some places referred to as a VLM or very large machine! This beast turns al the bottles at once and completes the process in just over a week.

Now we have a bunch of upside down wine bottles with a yeasty plug in the neck. So, with a practiced sleight of hand, or more likely in most cases another machine, the neck of the bottle is frozen, the cap pinged off, the plug of ice in the neck containing the lees shoots out and we just top up the bottle and bang in a cork. Again taking us back to the olden days that top up could be missed out and the emptiness was disguised by all that foil round the top of the bottle – yep that's where that idea came from. Now the top up will be with some extra wine and a dose of sugar to adjust the now dry wine in the bottle to the level of sweetness required. Most champagne is non-vintage (NV) denoting that the grapes do not all come from a single harvest, which is what we would expect given all that mixing of reserve wines and this is the same for rosé. So, are there vintage rosé champagnes to be had? Well of course – as I keep saying rosé is a proper wine so yes, many of the top champagne houses produce vintage rosés.

Bordeaux

I have mentioned Bordeaux a couple of times and this is hardly surprising as the region looms large over the whole world of wine. It is a reference point for winemakers wherever wine is made.

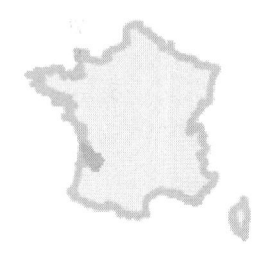

Although celebrated for its red wines Bordeaux is also a significant producer of rosé wines. These usually fall under the generic Bordeaux Appellation Controlé which stretches right across the region and permits wine to be made from grapes harvested anywhere within the region. This is not to say all the wine is made in some gigantic swimming pool, there are plenty of single estate wines of quality to discover and most AOC's in the region allow for rosé wines made from the same grapes as the mainstream red wines - Cabernet Sauvignon, Merlot, Cabernet franc, Malbec, Petit Verdot and Carmenere. Perhaps surprisingly Bordeaux accounts for 12% of the French rosé wine production.

Just to the south east of the classic Bordeaux region we get into Bergerac (please insert your own terrible detective reference here). This is in the Dordogne Département so you can imagine this is something which the English émigrés have thoroughly acquainted themselves with. Bergerac rosé is a fairly recent addition to the established red and white wines of the area. It is made mainly by the saignée method, although there is some use of the short maceration approach, producing a refreshing wine of a light salmon colour. It is also in the north of Bergerac in an amphitheatre of hills we find the charmingly named Rosétte wine which has its own AOC. This stands out for the other Bergerac wines being made from Sémillon, Sauvignon, and Muscadelle. If you look at that list and are thinking this might be little sweetie well you're right, it generally has around 45g/l residual sugar which is around 9 times what you would find in a dry wine. This is not by any means a sweet cloying wine, the sugar gives a rich mouth filling quality but retains enough acidity to be balanced and refreshing. The aromas are flowers and red fruits.

Burgundy

The other great winemaking region or perhaps region of great wines is Burgundy. Here production of Rosé is mainly left to the Beaujolais appellation.

Beaujolais made its name supplying the bouchons, or bistros, of Lyon. It is said that Lyon was built on three rivers the Rhône, the Saône and Beaujolais! The reason for the success was the pairing of this light fruity wine with the local appetite for charcouterie.

Some might argue a wine like Beaujolais Nouveau is more or less a rosé anyway as there is very rapid fermentation with very little maceration, albeit it does come out a distinct purple rather than pink colour. In fact Beaujolais Nouveau is made by a special technique called Carbonic Maceration whereby whole bunches are lobbed into a big tank and all the oxygen excluded so that an intracellular fermentation can take place within the grapes which then burst as they ferment. This makes for a very rapid extraction of colour but with very little tannin and preserves the fresh fruity nature of this young wine.

Well this is exactly how they do make rosé in Beaujolais! The only extra trick is that they take the free run juice to make the rosé then press the remainder to make Beaujolais as we know it. The wine is mainly made from Gamay grapes but the rules here allow up to 15% of other varieties in the blend including Aligoté, Chardonnay, Melon, Pinot Gris and Pinot Noir.

Rhone

The Rhone valley is really two regions for the price of one. In the north the valley is narrow and steep. This is the home of the peppery Syrah, also known as Shiraz, and the aromatic apricot aromas of Viognier. To the South the valley broadens out and so does the variety with Grenache, Carignan, Syrah, Bourboulenc, Calitor, Mourvèdre and Picpoul to name but a few. The famous Châteauneuf-du-Pape has something like 34 different permitted grape varieties in the blend!

However do not worry, amidst all this heavy hitting red wine there is also an AOC Côtes du Rhône Villages Rosé. This wine is 50% Grenache and at least 20% Syrah and Mourvèdre. In common with a lot of French appellations tagging Villages on the end means you are getting something that little bit better than the common or garden Côtes du whatever.

Whilst the North presents slim pickings for rosé fans in the south we have the appellation of Tavel on the right bank of the Rhone which is devoted to our cause as rosé is the only permitted style of wine. This is down to the union of vineyard owners and winemakers who in 1902 set about building the reputation of rosé wines by visiting all the most prestigious international wine fairs. However it was not until 1937 that the area was officially designated. The wine here seems even to prompt poetry in the French soul; Christophe Tassan said "Gorgeous Tavel dresses in a thousand shades of pink to seduce and captivate the senses. Luminous like no other wine, it inspires the chef, the eater and the eaten". Not quite sure "the eaten would agree with that!

Being further south the climate here is distinctly Mediterranean with an average of 2700 hours of sunshine each year. This favourable climate and the alluvial soils enables them to produce around 36,000 hectolitres of wine, about a quarter of which goes for sale abroad, so you should easily be able to find some☺ Appellations are all about rules and here they proscribe that 60% of the blend must be Grenache and 15% Cinsault, both well known as rosé friendly grapes, but after that they can pick and mix from a variety of varieties.

Next door is the denomination of Lirac. Lirac and Tavel are often paired together as a sort of Bonnie and Clyde of the southern Rhone. I would say that Lirac is definitely Clyde. Here across the four communes of Lirac, Saint-Laurent-des-Arbres, Saint-Géniès-de-Comolas and Roquemaure they make red, white and rosé wines but are particularly well known for their Rosé. The principal grapes are Grenache (at least 40%), Syrah and Mourvèdre (together at least 25%), Cinsault, Carignan (no more than 10%). Interestingly here they also allow white grape varieties up to a limit of 20% of the blend.

Lately the Cave Coop in Tavel, created in 1930' s , one of the first AOC's of France , was declared National Monument.

Despite the shining example of Tavel the Rhone region only makes up 14% of the French rosé production. Why would this be? Well, Baron Le Roy, one of the founders of the French AOC system, decided that Chateauneuf should get the right to make white and red , but not rosé otherwise he feared encouraging "brother killing" by the makers of Tavel, who were since the middle-ages already known for good rosé making.

Languedoc

Just before we reach the end of our journey let's take a rest in the Languedoc Roussillon region, after all many of us do on our holidays every year. This is an odd sort of region in that it is not a place the wine cognoscenti tend to talk about much – there is no equivalent of Chateau Petrus or Côte Rotie here. What there is though is an abundance of wine! The weather is more Mediterranean and very agreeable for growing grapes so that's what they do.

Go and check that odd bottle of French wine you picked up at the supermarket for £4.99 – where is it from? Does it perchance say Vin de Pays D'Oc on it? Well this is where it comes from then.

The good weather means they can get wine out of some of the tougher characters in the grape world which tend to be a little more rustic – such as Carigan. These are not fine wines but I find most wine is fine with me as long as I set my expectation meter correctly. These are quaffing wines, party wines, barbeque wines, picnic wines. This said the region does have AC regions and the wines to go with them but to me I think this is just maintaining due respect rather than aspirations of becoming the next Bordeaux. That respect was eroded back in the 1970's when much of the European wine lake was composed of surplus wine from here. But there are fine traditions as well – the French army rations in both world wars included Languedoc wine.

In terms of Rosé expect a simple fruity wine. There is a lot of Grenache used here which loves a bit of a baking in the sun and can produce a surprisingly high ABV. If it is not Grenache it is Cinsault (or a blend of the two!).

The region can though claim to host perhaps the most honest wine in the country – The Arrogant Frog! (Honestly this is done purely for the purposes of humour as I am a dedicated Francophile)

This is a 100% Syrah wine which promises cherries, toffee and candied fruit all for a surprisingly good price.

Provence

Perhaps I was saving the best until last. Provence is undoubtedly Rosé HQ! Here they produce more than 40% of French rosé wine and, as we have already mentioned, they have the CIVP which acts as a research centre and advocate of rosé wine in general and Provence in particular.

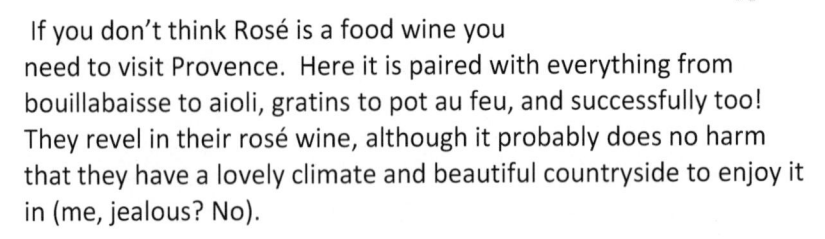

If you don't think Rosé is a food wine you need to visit Provence. Here it is paired with everything from bouillabaisse to aioli, gratins to pot au feu, and successfully too! They revel in their rosé wine, although it probably does no harm that they have a lovely climate and beautiful countryside to enjoy it in (me, jealous? No).

What did the Romans ever do for Provence? Well, they pitched up in the 2nd century and set about planting vineyards. The Phoenicians had started a lot earlier in Marseille but it is the |Roman legacy which had the greatest impact. The original hubs were the military port of Fréjus and the city

30

of Aquae Sextiae, now Aix en Provence. From here they went on to bring the joys of their civilisation, and their wine, to the Rhone, Beaujolais, Burgundy….but it started in Provence.

After the Romans it was the monks who continued to build the business and then come the 14th century nobility got in on the act. Today most of the rosé wine they produce is sold in France itself and nearly half of that right there in Provence.

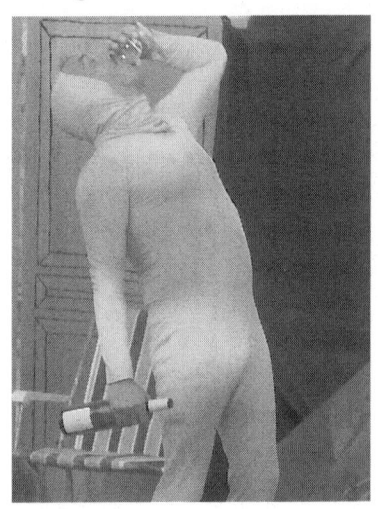

We all know how seriously the French take drinking wine!

As we have already seen Provence has no truck with the saignée method of making rosé but they choose instead either direct pressure or the short maceration we have already discussed. The direct pressure method is reserved for the lightest colour in the Provence palette, the Oiel de Perdix or partridge's eye. Most places in France this would probably be an appetiser to be eaten with a special pin but here in Provence it is a colour. The direct pressing of the grapes means the juice has very little skin contact and what there is, is cold so there is very little extraction of colour and tannin.

The Rosé Wine Research Council has come up with a scale of nine colours which are used to judge and classify Provencal wines - the colours are: Redcurrant, Rosewood, Raspberry, Flesh, Pink Marble, Salmon, Onion Skin, Brick and Coral. Now I for one would not be able pick pink marble or rosewood off a Dulux paint chart so fortunately for those who are real rosé geeks there is a kit of standard liquid colours in test tubes available.

Color Scale for Provence Rosé Wines

To paraphrase the immortal "Whispering Ted Lowe" for those reading in black and white the pink is just behind the other pink. Go to www.centredurose.fr for the full effect

If nine colours seems too extreme the CIVP have also defined their own colour chart for rosé wine. Here it is Gooseberry, Peach, Grapefruit, Cantaloupe, Mango and Mandarin which are the six names that have been attributed to the colours that are the most representative of Rosé Wines from Provence. As they say you pay your money and take your choice, although I have to say mango and mandarin sound more appealing than brick.

Rosés from Provence tend to be lighter and they back this up with some research by the CIVP which showed that consumers prefer lighter colours, while very few like dark-coloured rosés. Lighter wines are more floral and citrus in flavour with a hint of almonds whereas the darker wines are more about summer berries.

Anyway let's get something in a glass!!

The main grape varieties here are Grenache, Mourvèdre, Cinsault, Tibouren , and Syrah which must be 70% of the blend, rising to 80% from 2015. The wines are dry but not acerbic. The aromas may be fruity, floral or more herbaceous with mint and tobacco or even show some of the minerality of Chablis. The best are well rounded wines which will bring some complexity to the palate. Provence Rosé is not just a picnic glugger!

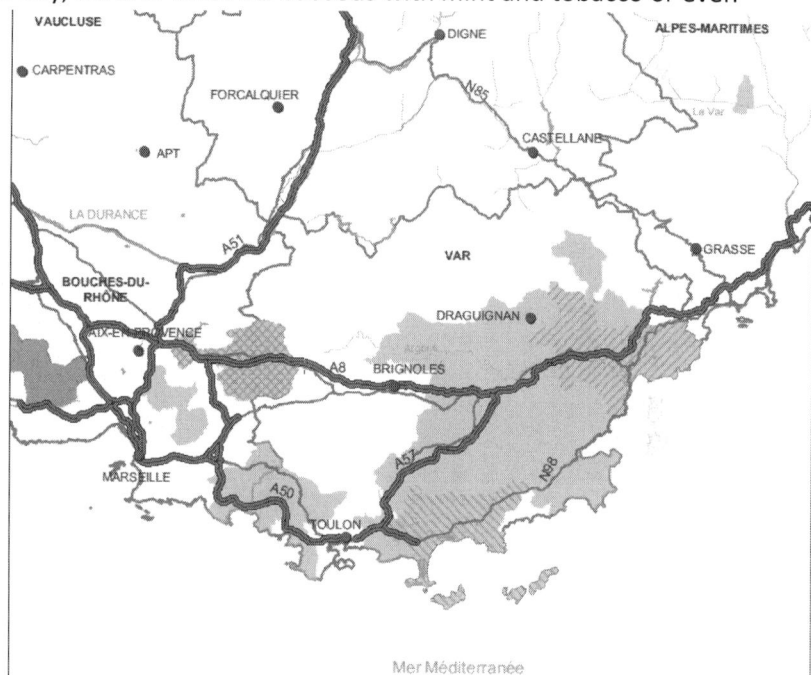

Around the appellations

There are 10 Official Appellations in Provence – Bandol,- Bellet, Cassis , Coteaux-d'Aix-en-Provence - Coteaux de Pierrevert , Cotes-de-Provence , Côtes de Provence, Sainte Victoire , Coteaux Varois , Les Beaux de Provence and Palette

Bandol - Rosés accounts for an ever increasing percentage of output, made from Cinsault, Grenache and Mourvedre.

Cassis– A small fishing village 20 kilometres east of Marseille. Although the AOC Cassis produces red, rosé, the main focus here is on white wines.

Bellet -An extremely small area with in a 30 minute drive north from Nice centre. Bellet has established a reputation for red, white and rosé wines. The rosés are supple, well structured, and fruity and will age well. The vineyards of Bellet are some of the oldest in France; originating with the arrival here of Phoenician Greeks.

Coteaux-d'Aix-en-Provence - A total of 49 communes make up the appellation of Coteaux-d'Aix-en-Provence producing mainly red, rosé wines. Most of the production concentrates on light and fruity rosé wines for early drinking.

Coteaux de Pierrevert This appellation includes 11 Villages across a total of 4,000 acres. About a third of the production is rosés.

Cotes-de-Provence The AOC Cotes de Provence is the largest in Provence and concentrates on the production of rosés. At their best the rosés are excellent, full of fruit, soft and aromatic. Sample some at the : **Maison des Vins-Rn7 83460 Les Arcs sur Argens, tel- 33 049 4995010.**

Côtes de Provence-Sainte Victoire This Appellation was regulated in 2005.

Coteaux Varois The wines are grown in 28 communes, all proud to showcase the new Coteaux Varois appellation awarded March

1993. Just over half the production here is rosé (Grenache and Cinsault).

Les-Baux-de-Provence
The AOC of Les Baux de Provence is limited to the production of red and rosés wines only and the strict AOC rules ensure that there is a quality output. The blend of grape varieties used is at least 60 % Grenache, Syrah, and Cinsault for rosés.

Palette
Palette is a very small vineyard, on the outskirts of Aix between the communes of Tholonet and Meyreuil and includes the respected estates of Château Simo.

Celebrity Wine

If you are looking to impress some friends why not go for a few bottles of Château Miraval. You probably won't be able to find this as the 6000 bottles sold out within hours as this is the wine made by Brad Pitt and Angelina Jolie in their little pied a terre in Provence. Well I say made by them I am not sure they tread the grapes themselves, although give the tradition is that this is done naked I may need to give that a little more consideration.

However if your friends are wine fans rather than devotees of Hello magazine go for Garrus from Château d'Esclans which is the most expensive still rosé wine you can buy.

However Château d'Esclans are also up to something else less prestigious in their "Sacha Lichine Single Blend". This contrary to what you might expect is not made at Château d'Esclans, nor yet in Provence but in nearby Languedoc.. And what is this single blend stuff about? Well to be a "single varietal" wine under EU regulations you actually only need 85% of whatever it is to make up the wine so it can quite legitimately be a blend and a single varietal at the same time. This wine is actually a Vin de France, so the bottom of the classification scale and is made from Grenache with a few bunches of Syrah and Cinsault. This does not mean it is bad wine but I think it raises an eyebrow or two.

Spain

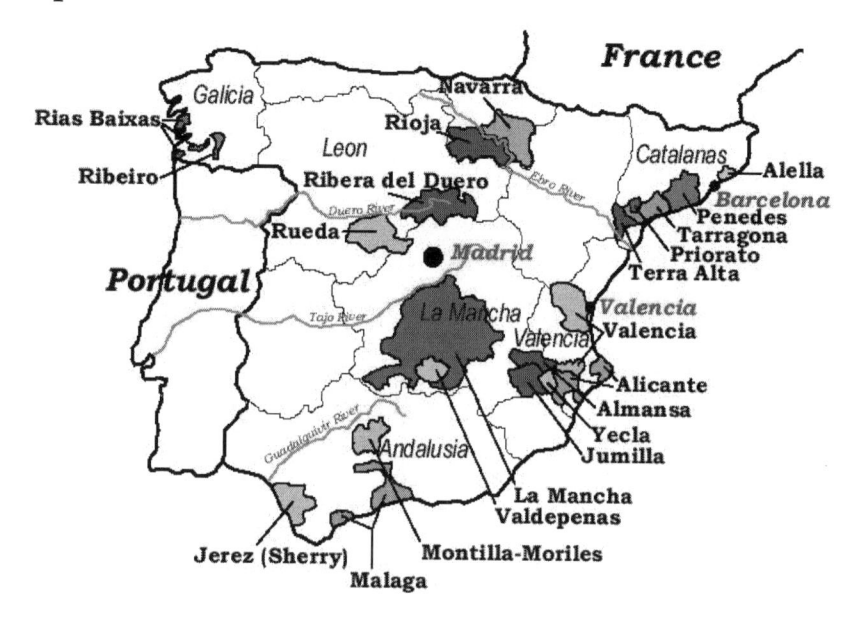

Map of Spain showing wine regions: Rias Baixas, Galicia, Ribeiro, Leon, Navarra, Rioja, Ribera del Duero, Rueda, Catalanas, Alella, Barcelona, Penedes, Tarragona, Priorato, Terra Alta, Madrid, La Mancha, Valencia, Alicante, Almansa, Yecla, Jumilla, Andalusia, Valdepenas, Jerez (Sherry), Montilla-Moriles, Malaga. Rivers shown: Duero, Ebro, Tajo, Guadalquivir.

Copyright: William Lembeck 2007

In Spain we are drinking *Rosado*. The home of many peoples favourite red wine, Rioja, is a wonderful location for the next stage of our world tour of Rosé. Spain is the third largest winemaker in the world behind France and Italy who battle it out for top spot. Having said which they are the country with the most acres (or hectares if you will) of land devoted to growing vines. Being further south it is generally hotter and drier than France and altitude has a particular role to play in selecting the right sites to grow vines. One of the reasons they have so much land under vines is that in the central region it is simply so hot and dry they have to space them out really far apart so each vine has enough resources to grow.

I have already alluded to the balancing act required to deliver a good rosé wine and in a hot place like Spain you are now on the high wire and juggling chainsaws. Overall the style is dry wines which will have a bit more of a punch to them. There are going to be some which disappoint but that is true of any region. Very few winemakers set out to make a bad wine but they may want to make a cheap wine and that is the end of the market that disappointment lurks.

Rioja

This is the headline wine of Spain and the region is one of only two holding the top accolade of Denominaciónes de Origen Calificada (DOCa), the other being Priorat. Other than these two top dogs there are some 65 Denominaciónes de Origen s (DO's) and after that we are mainly looking at table wines, Vino de la Tierra (VT's)For us the interest lies in the 15% of Rosado wine Rioja produces. The main black grapes here are Tempranillo, Garnacha (Grenache), Graciano (Carignan) and Mazuelo. For the rosados it is Garnacha and Tempranillo which take the lead.

Navarra

Rosé is produced around the country but Navarra, just to the North of the Rioja region, is the big player here, the Provence of Spain if you like. More than half the production of the region is Rosé wine and that wine is made from Garnacha, which is just their version of Grenache. This is a grape that loves heat and sunshine and has no time for rain – sounds like a grape you could be friends with? It also tends to make wines of quite a high alcohol content. There are other varieties allowed in the mix including Tempranillo which is the king of Rioja, this is joined by Graciano, Cabernet Sauvignon, Merlot and Carignan.

Penedès

Here we are in Catalonia just south of Barcelona. This is a fiercely independent region of Spain and they like to do things their own way. The style of many of the wines leans a little more toward leaving a touch of sweetness in the wine. There is also more use here of international grapes like Syrah, Merlot and Cabernet Sauvignon.

Penedès is also the home of Cava the Spanish sparkling wine made by the same methods as used in Champagne. This is a very jolly and enjoyable drink although does not generally have the finesse and yeasty/bready/biscuit notes of champagne. Yes, of course there is a rosé version ;-) Cava is generally made from a combination of Macabeo, Xarel-lo and Parellada grapes but in Conca de Barberà to the north of Tarragona province they use a native grape, Trepat. This is grown on soils called *licorella* which literally sparkle in the sunlight and are very similar to those of the prestigious DOCG region of Priorat. This wine brings you a glass of fresh strawberry and raspberry flavours with a hint of rosé petals.

The South East

In the Alicante and Jumilla DOs the winemakers have a very neat trick which is a bit like the Bordeaux producers getting two wines for price of one using the saignée method except they do it in reverse! This method, known as the *doble pasta* (meaning "double paste") takes the skins from the early pressed rosé wine and adds them to the red wine adding colour and depth to the wine by increasing the ratio of skins to juice just like they did in Bordeaux.

Portugal

winesbeersandspirits.com

Believe it or not Portugal leads the world in the consumption of wine per person at over 43l each! As an aside even more bizarre when it comes to the consumption of spirits it is South Korea who leads the way. But back to wine. It is perhaps a credit to Portugal that they have long been known for keeping all their best wine to themselves so despite the consumption figures they tend not to compete for the export podium places.

Now, hands up everyone who remembers Mateus Rosé? This was one of the quintessential drinks of the seventies. For those who don't remember this was a light rosé wine with a little sweetness and a little sparkle which came in a very distinctive bottle which your Mum made in to a table lamp.

The Mateus story goes back a bit further than this though to the middle of World War 2. Presumably with the idea of cheering a few people up two Portuguese winemakers both decided to make a sweeter sparkling wine aimed at the European and American markets. Fernando van Zeller Guedes was a winemaker from the Vino Verde region in the north of Portugal and had seen how well this wine, known for its freshness and sparkle, was selling in Brazil and figured if sweetened up would appeal to both the American and European markets. The rest as they say is history. The wine was named Mateus after the Mateus Palace which overlooks the Douro River that runs thought the northern wine regions of Portugal. Meanwhile further south José Maria da Fonseca in Setubal had a similar idea and started making his sparkling wine by the continuous method traditionally used for Making Asti Spumante in Italy. He targeted the American market fair and square with his wine called Lancers, which to rival the lovely Mateus bottle was packaged in a stoneware bottle. And so it is today, Lancers is what the Americans drink, and since its re-launch in 2005 Mateus is what we in Europe drink.

Douro Valley

The other drink Portugal is renowned for is of course Port and HQ is the Douro Valley. I see you are way ahead of me... yes, they do make Rosé Port.

Port takes its name from Oporto, the seaport where, since the 17th Century, British ships have brought back barrels to a thirsty nation. The British were so fond of the drink that families sent their sons to Portugal to become wine merchants and port producers.

There are many types of port including vintage, tawny, ruby and white. While some are aged for years in wood, or for decades in bottles, ruby port is aged for most of its three years in stainless steel or concrete vats. By port standards, it is young and meant to be drunk upon release.

Taylor-Fladgate in Vila Nova de Gaia which makes the very popular Croft brand was the first to make a rosé port in 2005 though others have now followed suit.

Port is a fortified wine and in this case the fermentation is stopped when there is a fair amount of residual sugar left. The stopping takes the form of adding distilled grape spirit to bring the alcohol level in the wine up to the point that the yeast gets killed off. Normally in making traditional port the challenge is to extract enough colour from the grapes in as short a time as possible because they want a really quick process so they can catch that residual sugar. There are all kinds of tricks to extract the colour form the skins including auto-vinifiers, piston plungers and now mechanical feet which mimic the action of treading the grapes in the traditional way, although without that cheesy note.

There are actually 29 permitted varieties of grape permitted in making port but Touriga Nacional, Touriga Franca and Touriga Roriz are the main ones. By the way this last one, Touriga Roriz, is just another name for our old friend Tempranillo.

So given the challenges of colour extraction making a Rosé port should be a fairly easy ride. It is made by combining the port and pressing techniques. Rosé port is in effect a ruby that has had light contact with the grape skins. The fruit is pressed as soon as possible to minimise the transfer of colour from the skins to the juice, leaving a rose-coloured must. This is then cold fermented and fortified like traditional port.

Typically rosé port combines the freshness and delicacy of rosé wine with the elegance and charisma of good port. Fine examples include Offley Rose Port, a Decanter Bronze medal winner, which is created from the red grape varieties Touriga Franca, Tinta Barocca and Touriga Nacional. It has a fine bouquet of tropical fruits and is fresh in the mouth with mango and guava flavours and a long elegant finish. Served in a large glass chilled or on the rocks and makes an excellent apéritif.

Quevedo Rosé is a young Port with a refreshing and smooth taste which describes itself as "cosmopolitan". This uses Touriga Nacional, Touriga Franca, and Sousão to produce flavours of ripe strawberry and raspberry fruit with hints of tropical fruits.

In common with most Rosé wines these ports are for drinking young, they are not something to lay down at your son's birth for celebrating his 21st.

Although other rosé wines from Portugal are hard to come across those that exist can hold their own against the best. At a taste test for the Italian Spirito Divine magazine, a rosé from Bairrada in the western part of the Beiras, between the mountainous Dão region and the surf-washed Atlantic. This wine, Colinas de São Lourenço Tête de Cuvée 2010, beat rosés from Italy, France and the UK. Achieving a very creditable 92/100 points it beat a Loire rosé with 88 points into second place.

Most of the rosé outside the ones mentioned so far come from the Baga grape. This is a native variety found in the Barraida region of central Portugal. Here it accounts for 90% of black varieties. This is a small, thin-skinned grape (baga means "berry" or "droplet" in Portuguese) which usually produces highly acidic, tannic wines when made in to red wine which are then of long aging. However, happily for us much of this grape is turned into rosé wine. Oh, and a large proportion of that is…Mateus Rosé!

Italy

Wikimedia Commons

Italy is arguably the world's largest wine producer with more vineyards even than France- although this is an argument chiefly contested by the French and Italians! The figures have them swapping places on regular basis. Whatever the precise numbers may be they produce a lot of wine.

Italian wine for me brings to mind the sour cherry flavours of red wine designed for Italian food and the (often) insipid flavours of Pinot Grigio which seems to be wine designed for people who do not really like wine but would like to have something vaguely refreshing and alcoholic in their glass. This is of course a view highly coloured by prejudice and has very little to support it (although I am not saying I am wrong). Italy has a fantastic wine story and many great wines to offer.

The story goes back to the Etruscans back in the fifth century BC who then passed the baton to the Romans who following the fine example of the Greeks before them dedicated a God of wine in Bacchus and started to develop a much more sophisticated wine culture. They found that they actually preferred wines which had aged, at least the ones which had been kept relatively airtight and not turned into vinegar. The wine of choice if you could afford it was Falernum which is mentioned in many Roman texts. Sadly somewhere along the road from antiquity the recipe was lost.

The ancient wines of Rome would often be watered down to make them palatable, or mixed with herbs and honey to make Mulsum. Some especially acidic wines even had chalk added by the drinkers - a trick you may like to try on an acerbic house red next time you are in an Italian restaurant.

Anyway enough history, do they make rosé? Would I be writing about them if they didn't?

Believe it or not they make a Pinot Grigio rosé. The PG grapes are actually a lightish pink in colour so with a typical 12 hour maceration they can produce a very pale *oeil de la perdix* wine which would feel right at home in Provence.

Italy has always been a loose association of areas which cultivate a distinct feeling of place, just think back to the original city states. It's no surprise then to learn there is a "pink divide". In the North, home of the Pinot Grigio pink wine is indeed rosé but in the south it is Rosato.

Although it is a distinct minority interest Italy has a wine fair devoted to rosé wines every year in Moniga del Garcia. This little town on the western shores of Lake Garda started what they hope will be a grand tradition in June 2012 of the "Italia in Rosa" festival.

Set in the grounds of the Villa Bertanzi visitors are treated to more than 100 Italian wineries being represented, both still and sparkling.

USA

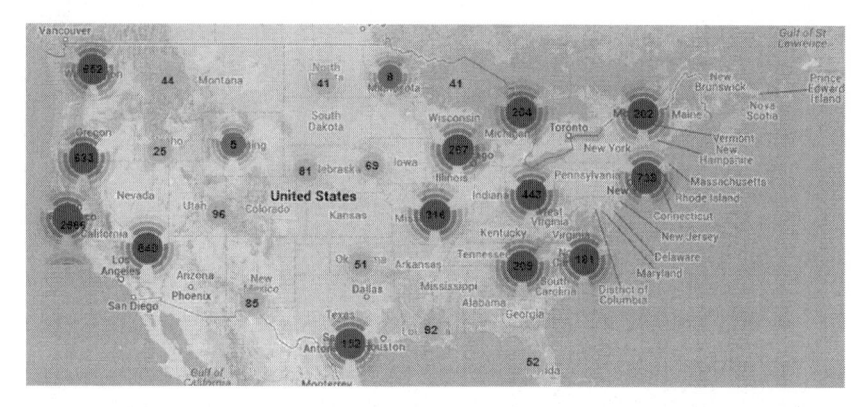

Just to show US wine is not just about California (although it mostly is!)

In the USA, and California in particular, you will find almost every variety of grape being grow in every possible way and being made into every type of wine! They just love to experiment and there are around 7,000 commercial wineries doing just that. I can only think it's something to do with the pioneer spirit. Anyway, what this means for us is that they produce some fantastic rosé wines.

In the USA though they have a particular trick up their sleeve in the form of what they call blush wines which are generally a pale but definite pink. More confusing still is the Zinfandel, the rosé version of which they refer to as white Zinfandel - confused? Well, there is a story I need to tell you....

Once upon a time in the west, well, in southern California in 1972, the Sutter Home vineyard was doing great business with what they thought of as their signature grape - black Zinfandel. This they used to make a powerful red wine which was going down very well with the locals and everyone else who got a taste of it. However they wanted to go one better and produce an even more intense deeply coloured wine. The winemaker, Bob Trichero, hit on the idea of using the Bordeaux technique of bleeding the red wine to increase the ratio of skins to juice. This left him with 550 gallons of white grape juice. He was persuaded to make some wine as a curiosity to split between the Sutter Home tasting room and a Conti Brothers grocery in Sacramento. Initially Bob was thinking chardonnay style and fermented this to dryness. This was interesting but did not set the world alight. Then in 1975 disaster! The fermentation just stopped with 2% residual sugar left in the wine. Well, it was a busy time of year and the wine just got left in the fermenter. Two weeks later and it had also turned a light pink. So, it got bottled anyway and the rest as they say is history. From Now it turned out that one year they just had a really enormous harvest and more grapes than they knew what to do with. OK they thought "let's make some pink wine - it's pretty hot around here and something a bit lighter might go down well". So they made the first batch of white zinfandel in the classic short maceration style. Then they stopped the fermentation before it was finished so not all the sugar was converted to alcohol and they filtered off the result (filtering takes out the yeast so the wine cannot change its mind later and start fermenting again which apart from anything else would mean an embarrassing number of exploding bottles!). What do you know the light sweet strawberry flavoured wine leapt off the shelves.

Nice as it is white zinfandel is one of the reasons so many people do not believe that rosé wine is anything but a light sweet frivolous alcopop. Of course the USA has a lot more to offer than this and in the North around Washington and Oregon we are looking at classic Pinot Noir rosés, dry and crisp.

In New York State around Finger Lakes they produce a variety of wines but you need to be wily to understand what you are getting in the bottle. In the USA there are various tiers of regulation applying the declared America Wine Areas, to states and to regions. In New York State a "local" wine may only contain 45% New York wine with 35% coming from added sugar and water and 25% wine from elsewhere.

California

Arguably Californian wine is American wine as 90% of US production comes from the sunshine state.

California made a potentially inauspicious start to the current wine era ten years ago with what was known as "two buck chuck" – jug wines that were a series of varietal wines made by Charles Shaw which were originally sold in Trader Joe's supermarket. Although truth be told apparently it was not a bad drop. However this is not the image of California today. Now it contends with the best wine making regions of the World.

The state is some 1100 kilometres long North to South so they have plenty of opportunity to try different climates. This is helped by the variety of valleys and ocean breezes. In fact it gets quite complicated so the University of California has evolved a classification system which splits the state into five so called "Davies zones" after the Davies campus of the university where the winemaking faculty is based. In the hotter areas to the south grapes ripen quickly and can produce wines which are high in alcohol and lacking in acidity, especially where Grenache leads the blend. However these are quite suitable conditions for the blush wines which remain popular

Sparing the blushes they do make some "serious" rosé here which tend towards the dry or off dry . It used to be that this was made on a non-commercial basis for personal use by the winemakers but since it took off ten years ago Rosé has been at the front of the shop rather than the back. The better areas are to the north so look out for names like Russian River, Carneros and Dry Creek Valley.

Production methods embrace Saingnée , Pressing and Maceration, and as in other places there are arguments about what is the "proper" method. I say interesting as it is to know how it got there what counts most is what you taste in the glass.

Pinot Noir as ever is a popular candidate grape along with other classic varieties like Syrah, Grenache and Cinsault.

A fine example of the new rosé which was singled out by the Los Angeles Times is the 2012 Bonny Doon Vineyard Vin Gris de Cigare. This is a Vin Gris made from 62% Grenache, 17% Mourvèdre, 9% Roussanne, 6% Grenache blanc, 6% Cinsault which are grown specifically for making this wine, so not leftovers from red wines, and harvested only just ripe to preserve the acidity. As a Vin Gris there is minimal skin contact so this is a pale pink wine. Then after fermentation there is extended lees contact which creates a creaminess and smooth texture. The nose is of alpine strawberry, with notes of blood orange, and grapefruit evolving into a refreshing mintiness with additional air and warming. This is set within a lean, mineral-intensive structure which makes this more sophisticated than simpler fruity wines.

Chile

Vancouver International Wine Festival • © 2012

Chile is a great country for good value wine. Although the wine growing region is seldom more than 50Km wide it is 1000Km long so there is the opportunity for plenty of variation. Now we are in the Southern hemisphere we need to remember that North is hot and south is cold. Of at least equal influence are the mountain ranges, mainly here for their effect on the climate rather than altitude.

Seeing the opportunity here several French and Spanish producers, such as Chateaux Margeaux and Concha y Toro, have set up operations in Chile to take advantage of not just the growing conditions but also the favourable economic climate. It may have been home to the odd revolutionary in its time but they which side their bread is buttered.

Wine growing here was introduced in the sixteenth century when Cortés ordered Spanish colonists to plant 1000 vines for every 100 dead Indians. Happily this system has been retired for some time! Following independence in 1850 they turned to French vines and winemakers who established what has now become a thriving wine industry.

Incidentally a lot of the grapes produced go to the production of the national spirit, Pisco. I recall being mightily impressed by a colleague from Peru who would not travel without his own cocktail shaker which he would use to make Pisco sours as he could not trust foreigners to do it justice!

Understandably many of the wines are based on classic French varieties, no bad thing in a market where being a well-priced bottle saying "Chardonnay" is likely to get you off the shelf in double quick time.

A couple of the reasons wines are well priced is cheap land and cheap labour. This is why Chile is also an outstanding example of Fair Trade Wine. The Fairtrade foundation in effect "kite marks" producers who ensure a fair deal for the workers, often now a cooperative. This will include paying the farmers a fair price and ensuring education for the children as opposed to simply being field hands at the right height for picking grapes. The wine is just as good and to me tastes a little better knowing the shares in the price are being more fairly distributed. So to the Rosé! First recommendation - I cannot recall ever having a bad one from here.

Wines here are from the dry end of the spectrum and you can find plenty made form classic read grapes making for a wine with a bit of character. The angelically named Cherub by Montes is a good example made from Syrah (Syrah rather than Shiraz tells you they mean it to be classy!).

By contrast in every way is Casillero Del Diablo Shiraz Rose made by Concha Y Toro in the Rapel valley region. The name literally means the Cellar of the Devil! Don Melchor de Concha y Toro, a Chilean statesman, entrepreneur and vineyard owner started the business in the late 1800s. He brought vines from Bordeaux and planted them on his estate. He created the legend of the Casillero del Diablo when he discovered that some of his best wines were being stolen from his cellar. Don Melchor spread the rumor that his deepest cellars were haunted by the devil. That's where he put his best wine, and the thefts stopped.

Anyway the wine is here proclaiming its colours by saying Shiraz and is a bolder spicier glass than the cherub.

Miguel Torres, one of the biggest producers, has a range of fair trade wines under the name Santa Digna including a Cabernet Sauvignon rosé. This is made in the Central Valley in Chile which is where most of the production is so makes good example to get to know Chilean wine. This one offers perfumed notes of plum and strawberry with hints of grapefruit. For a rosé it is full-bodied with well balanced acidity.

Argentina

Uncork Life! Blog Copyright © 2009

Neighbour to Chile but very different in many ways it is the availability of altitude that gives Argentina the means to make wines as they choose.

Like everywhere else Vinos Rosados are getting increasingly popular in Argentina but they are still playing second fiddle to the reds. Before the rise in popularity this was one of those places where rosé literal was a case of take a bottle of red and a bottle of white – hey presto two bottles of rosé. Now this is something you only reserve for the wines that are not going to cut it on their own so not surprisingly the rosé wine produced like this was pretty poor. Today they are made using the traditional methods and fermented under temperature control to produce wines which can now think about taking a serious part in the battle for our pink pound.

Argentina is the place where they have raised Malbec to cult status producing well ripened attractive wines through their use of irrigation and altitude. This is not the Malbec of Cahors in France, so woody and tannic you expect to get splinters off it! Good as it is at current prices it is great value as well. Given that Malbec is what they know they also use this in their rosé wines.

Mendoza is the region leading the way in rosé production and given the use of Malbec and demand for a more sophisticated wine than the sweet glugger it is not surprising they predominantly produce wine in a drier style which has aromas and flavours of dark cherries and black fruits. Syrah is also likely to find its way into many of the blends and generally we are looking at something towards the darker end of the rosé colour scale. With the structure and dryness imparted from these classic grapes this is a rosé you can pair with grilled meats and stews.

However Argentina does have breadth to its offering as well. In San Juan province we see Pinot Noir and Cabernet Sauvignon being employed to make lighter more aromatic styles. A particularly appealing move is the blending of some Torrontes to bring some floral notes to the wine. Torrontes is the Argentinean white grape to the Malbec's black grape. I know we are not talking about white wine here but do take the opportunity to try some Torrontes next time you see it.

Australia

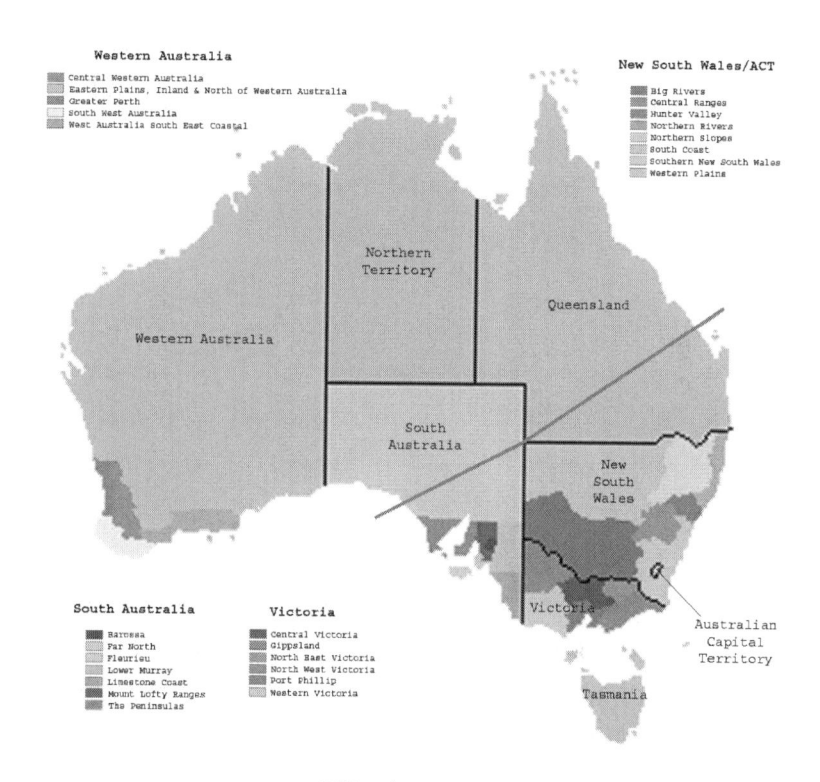

Western Australia
- Central Western Australia
- Eastern Plains, Inland & North of Western Australia
- Greater Perth
- South West Australia
- West Australia South East Coastal

New South Wales/ACT
- Big Rivers
- Central Ranges
- Hunter Valley
- Northern Rivers
- Northern Slopes
- South Coast
- Southern New South Wales
- Western Plains

South Australia
- Barossa
- Far North
- Fleurieu
- Lower Murray
- Limestone Coast
- Mount Lofty Ranges
- The Peninsulas

Victoria
- Central Victoria
- Gippsland
- North East Victoria
- North West Victoria
- Port Phillip
- Western Victoria

Wikimedia Commons

Australia is well known as the home of the value for money, fruity, friendly bottle of wine. We still think of them as new world but the first vines were planted in 1787 by Captain Arthur Phillips. This though was a hopeless failure as the vines were infected and promptly died! But that indomitable spirit of the continent was alive and well even then and three years later they had another go and established the first vineyard at Parramatta.

Over more recent years though there have been a few changes. First of all the quality has improved markedly and now rivals the best in the (old) world. They still have appealing styles but these have adapted to our own increasingly sophisticated tastes. They have like all of us suffered with the general economic recession which has hit the wine business the same as everyone else, and bear in mind they have to ship their wine a jolly long way to reach anyone. However one of the hardest blows has been climatic, in short water. In the more arid areas of South East Australia where the supply from the Murray/Darling river systems has been failing the competition for water is coming down to people or grapes some years, and understandably grapes have been losing out. In 2007 the big drought halved grape production.

However they do still manage to produce wines on a terrific scale in the wide open spaces of South East Australia. Yellow Tail for example is a terrifically popular brand and produces more wine in a year than the entire output of Portugal.

The sort of a growing appetite for Rosé has been repeated in Australia just as we have seen everywhere else. This said Aus' is not well known for rosé wines and a lot of the production tends to be of the sweeter fruitier variety similar to that seen in California, although there are some producers who have moved in to drier styles often based on Pinot Noir or the Italian Sangiovese.

A good friend who specialises in what she calls "Woof, woof" wines was persuaded to try the rose option - here is an insight into the reactions of a dedicated Red Wine drinker...

> "With trepidation, we attacked the "Rose of Virginia" by renowned Aussie Wine make base d in the yummy Barossa region, Charles Melton. 2006 vintage, it has clearly been stashed away in the Transtherm (Wine fridge) for a year or two too many for a pinko and will be well over. But never mind, we'll try anyway.
>
> We unscrewed the cap .... its a gorgeous ruby or bright pink colour - it's immediate nose was a shade musty - redolent of a Cab Sav whiff - but opens into strawberry, raspberry and cranberry with a hint of vegetal aromas - mushroom, perhaps

raspberry leaf and definitely a bit of blackcurrant leaf, unmistakably the cab sav smell vibe going on.

On the palate, the clean medium plus intensity (for a rose!) flavours burst on the tongue - fresh raspberries, strawberries and sweet ripe red cherries , along with sour cherry juice. Is it developing STILL? Surely not a 2006 Rose! It tastes fresh, vibrant and is just delicious, inviting you to sip more (don't mind if I do). For a rose, I'd call this full bodied but that's probably not on the scale either.

*The wine - 50% grenache, 43% Cab, 3.5% Pinot Meunier and 3.5% shiraz is a delicious joy, which I think you would *love* - the full on joy of a proper woof woof, but pink!*

And to think that was lurking in the fridge when you were over and you've missed out. I've checked I am afraid and it's the only one I had! Having a quick squiz via wine tracker just now, the 2010 got 90 points so it might be worth hunting that one out.

Dead, dead surprised that it's been such a keeper but when you look at the grape content, of course not ... Anyway. Thanks for making us drink it."

Mags Rivett

So let's have a quick spin around the country and see what's going on...there may be a woof waiting for us!

Barrossa Valley and McLaren Vale

Here they are manly planting Grenache for their rosé. Given the climate this comes out rather like boiled lollies and summer fruits.

Western Australia

These guys have only about 5% of the growing area in the country but will joyfully tell you they take 30% of the awards, so they musty be doing something right. It is the HQ for Cabernet Sauvignon production, especially around Margaret river. This being the case of course what do they use for their rosé but Cabernet Sauvignon.

Understandably given the reputation of the area the quality here is consistently good although the wines are a little lighter and sweeter than you might expect for a CS based rosé.

Yarra Valley

Yarra Valley stands out as being a producer of both still and sparkling rosé wines. Here they are using the Pinot Noir and making a drier more classical wine with flavours of plum and spice.

Adelaide Hills

Here the climate is a little cooler and the style of wine is the drier brisker style of the South of France. Here the varieties are mainly Cabernet Sauvignon and Pinot Noir which are handled to produce quite delicate wines. Yes, of course Australians can do delicate!

Mudgee

Here it all gets rather bold and experimental. Classic varieties and Italian imports all run shoulder and the wines are ripe and savoury.

David Fesq, a noted commentator on Australian wines, singles out one wine in particular for praise in the new rosé revolution, that is the Between Five Bells Geelong Rosé. This has seven varieties of white and black grapes including Zinfandel, Shiraz, Muscat and Chardonnay. Production is more like a red wine than the more usual white wine route for rosés. They allow a fair amount of oxidation to occur, which would normally be anathema, Fermenting and aging the wine in oak. The result has more than a hint of orange about it but is dry and moreish with flavours of peach and strawberry. Sad to say I have not managed to track down a bottle but if you do have a slurp for me - it sounds like an experience!

New Zealand

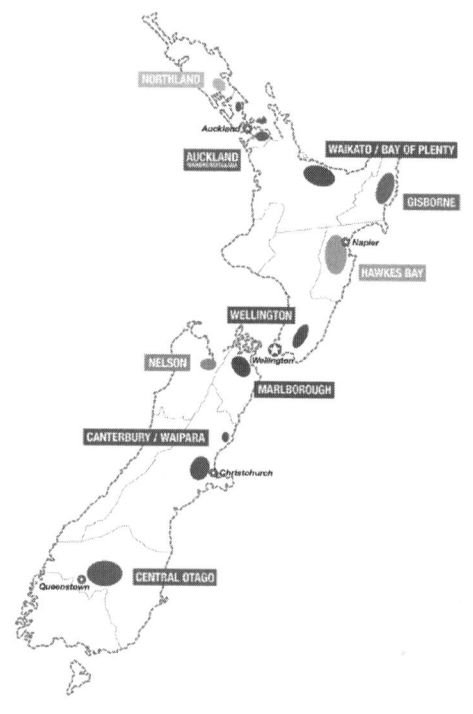

Wikimedia Commons

New Zealand is best known for its almost definitive production of Sauvignon Blanc which many would even say eclipses the French expression of this wine. Being almost the wine antipodes of France they have also mastered the Cabernet styles of Bordeaux and a most sophisticated Rhone like style of Syrah than their Australian cousins version of big "woof, woof" shiraz wines. But as I hope you are coming to realise, where there is wine there is rosé.

Granted in New Zealand there is not that much of it but as with red and white wines what there is has been made with exceptional care concentrating on quality rather than quantity.

Even with this limited canvas they manage to produce a range of rosé styles though. In Martinborough on the North Island the Vynfields winery produces a pale pink wine in the Oeil de Perdix, or eye of the partridge, style of Provence. The wine is called Peche de Noir - so peaches from black grapes, here the ubiquitous Pinot Noir. The wine is bone dry but unusually for a rosé is aged in oak barrels. However we are talking here about old oak not new so this is about resting the wine and allowing a tiny amount of oxidation rather than the addition of vanilla and toasty flavours associated with new oak.

Air New Zealand sponsors an annual wine competition which includes a rosé category, which I like to think is a significant sign that the Kiwis are taking rosé as a serious wine. In 2011 there were 15 medal winners in the rosé section, including the attractively named Blushing Monk, but sadly only one gold medal. That gold went to 8 Ranges Pinot Rosé from Central Otago. This is the central region of the South Island which has a decidedly continental climate whereas the other wine producing areas of the country are much more maritime, indeed Bordeaux-like. This means a hotter drier growing and ripening season which ensures grapes which reach full maturity and have a good concentration of sugar which means the winemaker has some great raw material to work with.

South Africa

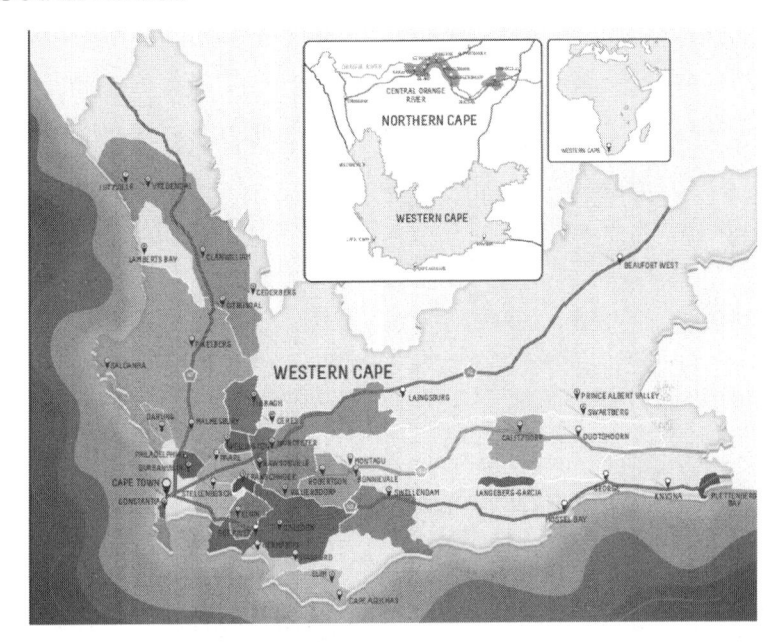

Wines of South Africa

South Africa is another of those very old new world locations having been making wine since 1659. It founded its reputation curiously enough on a sweet wine, Constantia, which is made just down the road from Cape Town. In its heyday this was the wine preferred by the European courts to the likes of Chateau Yquem, Tokay, and Madeira.

Having had a rather chequered political history much of the production in South Africa has always been based around cooperatives. Back in the seventies and eighties South African Wine was synonymous with KVW which operated a sort of national cooperative of five wineries. Since the end of apartheid cooperatives have evolved as more of a community based endeavour and several operate under the Fair Trade banner ensuring that money is invested back into the still achingly poor communities where they are based. The South Africa Fairtrade label was established as a non for profit organisation in 2008 and a year later affiliated to the international Fairtrade Organisation.

The greatest change has been the programme of Black Economic Empowerment which was established by Nelson Mandela's government to ensure that the new economy of South Africa would be one that valued the contribution of all the people and gave opportunity to the black majority to play a full role in that development.

Pinotage is really the signature grape of South Africa. Others have tried to grow it but on the whole have failed to make it deliver with only New Zealand somehow managing to coax a decent brew out of it. The classic flavours of Pinotage are rather earthy, even some would say a bit reminiscent of compost! This sounds pretty uninviting but somehow combined with the fruitiness of mulberry, blackberry and damson the wine it creates a savoury flavour which makes you keep coming back for more. Pinotage is a cross between Pinot Noir and Cinsault. Now there are a couple of grapes we have met a few times - both are widely used for producing rosé wines. Although it is a minority pursuit Pinotage makes some delicious rosé wines which are full of strawberry fruit and an edge which gives them some interest. Indeed some, the revered Oz Clarke included, say that rosé may be the way forward for capitalising on the strengths of Pinotage which can prove to be a bit of a handful when producing a full blooded red wine. Karien Lournes of Anchor Yeast writing in the South Africa wine trade publication Wynboer agrees; she suggests that many Pinotage producers would make a far better rosé than they produce red. One reason for this is that there is a problem here with virus infection particularly of red fruiting vines which means that they can struggle to reach that full ripeness which is so highly valued, but is not required when the objective is a dry rosé.

You may think from the origins of South African wine they may have bit of a sweet tooth here and you would be right, a lot of the rose made in South Africa follows the lead of the US blush style - light, fruity and medium sweet. The fruit tends to be picked quite late so the grapes have fully reached their sugar ripeness, even on occasion gone over into concentrating the sugar through drying or even noble rot. There has been a recent increase in the drier styles but this has yet to take off in the domestic market where the choice is generally for a white wine when otherwise rosé may fit the bill.

Celebrity Wine

They also have their own celebrity wine makers joining in the party. The Parlotones have produced three wines to date "Push me to the floor", "Giant mistake" and "We call this dancing", the last of which was a rosé they produced in 2010. Their lead singer Kahn Morbee modestly described it in the following purple rather than rosé prose "This wine will transport you to a place of romance lying in a strawberry field with a pale pink sunset as your backdrop as you sip on rose petals, raspberries, melted marshmallows and watermelon".

South Africa also has their own special version of fizz which is called Cap Classique. This is produced in the traditional champagne method although does not seem to quite capture the same yeasty notes as the original.

Germany

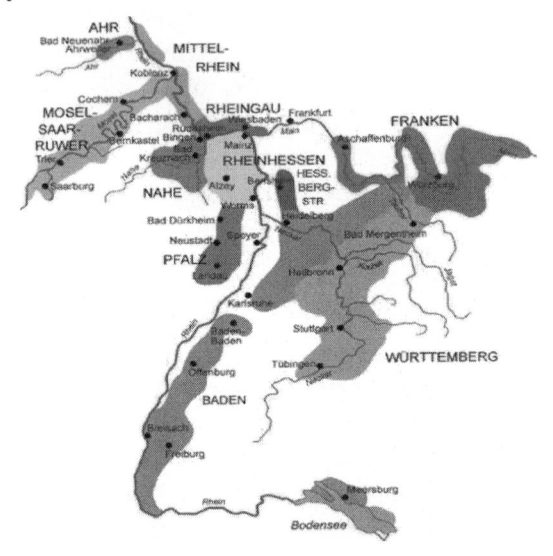

German Wine USA

Germany is renowned for easy drinking whites, generally a little on the sweeter side but this is only the very tip of the German wine iceberg. They have a comprehensive array of wines which for some reason never seem to make it beyond their borders. Oh, now I remember why – they drink them all themselves. Granted it is no France, but they have their own sparkler called Sekt which is a nice light quaffing drink. In fact Germans are the largest consumers of sparkling wine in Europe according to the 2013 Vinexpo survey. They have reds mainly produced in Baden from Pinot Noir, called here Spätburgunder, and Dornfelder, and they have dry whites mainly made in the north east in Franconia.

A German gentleman points out how well I am taking to their wine

Did I miss something? Ah yes, they have some fine rosé wines, or rosewein auf Deutsche , one of which you can see me drinking in Bonn – a cheeky little off dry Pinot Noir. In fact the Germans seem to like rosé almost as much as they like sparkling wine and are the third largest consumers after France and the USA.

Apart from the classic Pinot Noir which one finds almost everywhere the Germans have their own particular varieties from which they make rosés from bone dry to diabetes in a glass!

Blauer Portugieser, a central Europe grape whatever the name implies, makes some fresh simple rosés. Blaufrankisch is a little spicier and more floral. Then there is Dornfelder which is actually well known for red wines and is often used in blends to beef up the colour quotient. Fuchs Weingut (winery) in Rheinhessen make a light press wine with Dornfelder which comes out at the sweeter end of the spectrum with quite low alcohol as a consequence. This is fairly typical of the Dornfelder rosés and caters for the German taste for something with a degree of sweetness to it.

In terms of quantity and in my view quality it is the Spätburgunder, Pinot Noir, which wins through. They get plenty of practice as well as Germany is also the third largest grower of Pinot Noir I the world.

United Kingdom

At least I can write that now and know that precious few people will now be biting into their cigar and declaiming "English wine! Whatever next?". Yes, English wine has come a long way. So far it is actually now undergoing a further revolution. Many of the vineyards which were set up in the sixties and seventies growing German varieties and new crosses which had some slim chance of ripening in the limpid UK sunshine are now being rethought, especially in the south of England. Given the climate really has changed, and the chalky south downs are actually geologically the same stuff as you find in champagne a number of growers are now grubbing up the old vines and planting, you guessed it, the champagne varieties of Chardonnay, Pinot Noir and Pinot Meunier.

Wine tasting at home in Hampshire

In my own neck of the woods Hambledon Vineyard is just coming to the point in a ten year programme of investment which will see them producing English sparkling wine in really commercial quantities from their state of the art winery. This is down to the faith, insight, determination and outrageously persuasive owner XX. He must be persuasive to have got the investment this has taken with no output to speak of for so long. However it has been worth the wait and they are producing English Sparkling wine which rivals, and betters, the French version. So much so Nyetimber, another nouveau English winery in 2012 beat the French at their own game.

Most English winemaking is relatively small scale

Well, all of this is a bit of an aside. Although I have yet to taste a really good, well even nice, English red I have tasted many excellent English Rosé wines (and for once I rise above the temptation at a weak punning allusion!)

English rosés will generally owe their genesis to the Dornfelder, Rondo or Pinot Noir grapes. The first two are crosses which come to us from Germany; well coloured and capable of ripening here but for me the flavour leaves something to be desired. Pinot Noir though is another kettle of fish. This is the grape of Gevrey-Chambertin and Nuits St Georges so what is it doing in Merrie England? Well a bit like chardonnay this old soak will turn up to the party anywhere it hears a cork being pulled. Germany, whose clothes we are constantly stealing in terms of grape varieties, is actually the third largest producer of Pinot Noir after France and USA, so why not England?

Although quite a few modern Pinot Noirs are well up the rich, well oaked scale if left to its own devices it makes quite a light red so it is a small step to take to move this into the area of rosé whilst carrying a lot of the natural character with you.

At Jenkyn Place in Hampshire Simon Bladon replaced hop fields with vines and in 2009 they late picked their Pinot Noir and made a red wine, just so that they could bleed it for a sparkling rosé. This is another example of the march of English sparkling wine; a glass of wild strawberry and cherry with some hints at floral notes, delightful.

Wines and Grapes

Throughout the book various grape varieties have been popping up left right and centre so this is a another "I'm in a hurry give me some facts" section for everyone tired of the meandering discursive style (a bit like this so get on with it!!).

Here are the main grape varieties used in the production of rosé wines and what you might expect of them.

Pinot Noir

Widely used to produce rosé around the world, almost always by the short maceration method. Strawberry, cherry, perhaps a hint of something gamey. The good ones are *very* good - why not try an English example.

Pinotage

Really only of significance so far in South Africa. Strawberry and raspberry fruit with a hint of grassiness.

Gamay

Mainly found in France although has made some impression in Italy and California. Almost always ion a blend here it brings raspberries and a hint of pear. Go for a French example.

Cabernet Franc

This mostly appears in a blend, usually with Gamay and Malbec. Also make an appearance in Cabernet d'Anjou a first cousin to Rosé d'Anjou and usually a little drier. Raspberries with hint of blackcurrant leaves after the rain.

Cabernet Sauvignon

Particularly used where they are known for red wines and the winemaker bleeds off the juice to make a rosé. Blackcurrant is the signature flavour although expect this to be more subtle in a rosé. Bordeaux Rosé is the one to go for.

Merlot

Another classic grape which has the highest credentials for red wine making but which also makes a superb dry rosé with blackberry fruit and the structure to hold up to food.

Zinfandel

Also known as Primitivo in Italy. In the USA especially this is the grape of the blush wine. Generally sweet and low in alcohol with a crowd pleasing strawberry hit. Try Sutter Home Blush.

Cinsault

Sometimes rendered Cinsaut. This is the grape of the south and especially Langedoc in France. Best known for its contribution to Lirac and Tavel wines as well as the Cotes de Provence alongside the Grenache. The tough skins are rarely damaged by machine harvesting. It was used for many years as a table grape. It gives the wine a fresh, fruity touch but its basic harshness should be mitigated by the other grapes in the blend. Go with a Cotes de Provence for the full on bone dry rosé experience with subtle flavours.

Shiraz

Also known as Syrah in France and when the producer wants to sound more up market. In the South of France termed a *"cepage ameliorateur"* or grape blend improver. These small, black grapes with bluish highlights are known for making big reds this makes a fine full bodied dry rosé with a little tannin, good fruit and can be a very satisfying wine although unlikely to have the pepper of a bold red. Produces full-bodied rosés

Grenache

Also known as Garnacha in Spain. Widely used in the blends of Coteaux d'Aix-en-Provence appellation where it imparts a light, orangey tint to the local rosés. This variety gives young wine elegant aromas red berries; as it ages, develops spicier notes with increased body and richness. The best examples come from hillside vineyards.

Although a vital element in many Rhone wines where it provides flavour and alcohol Spain grows more of this than anyone else. A taste of dusty raspberries and a hint of earthiness although cheap ones will disappoint.

Grolleau

Also known as Groslot. The grape of Anjou Rosés and very little else. A great picnic wine which given its sweetness takes especially well to chilling which can rob some other rosé wines of any taste at all.

Malbec

Also known as Cot in France and Auxerrois in Cahors itself. Really shines in its expression in Argentina where it makes excellent red and rosé wines. Dry, a hint of tannin and dark cherry fruit even a hint of violets.

Rosé and Food Matching

I once heard someone talking about matching food with wine refer to rosé as the "beer of wine world" because it goes with everything. I think there is some truth in this and there is a lot of fuss about food and wine matching which feels like it is just overspill from wine snobbery. However, there are some combinations which enhance the food and the wine, and there are others which make can make both taste pretty frightful!

You will have heard some of the classics - Port and stilton, Sherry and almonds, Sauternes and Foie Gras. They are classics for a reason, they work. There is an old saying in the wine trade, which I am fairly sure I did not make up, "sell on cheese, buy on an apple", on the principle, especially with red wines, cheese will soften and flatter a wine whereas the acidity in an apple will show up its weaknesses.

So how does rosé fit into this picture? Well by now I am hoping you will realise not all rosés are created equal. They may be dry or sweet, firm or supple, still or fizzy. So here is my rough guide to matching them with foods

Salty foods - they may not be good for the blood pressure but salt does wonders for wine. It gives a wine more body making it seem smoother and richer. It also offsets dryness and bitterness. Go for a dry rosé like a Merlot or even a Malbec.

Fatty foods - fat tends to offset the acidity in a wine and give your palate a feeling of being cleansed. Go for a wine with high acidity otherwise it may end up tasting a bit dull and flabby. Something like a Rosé Pinot Grigio or a pale Provencal rosé.

Savoury foods - thee are foods with the Umami taste you get with cooked mushrooms, tomatoes and take away Chinese food. The best bet here is to go with something very fruity with no tannins so a light rosé is a good choice. This works well with chilli heat which increases the sensation of bitterness and the burn form alcohol so a low ABV is the one to go for unless you enjoy that particular thrill!

Chicken, Pork, Veal (Rose veal naturally) all go well with a dry or off dry rose depending on the sauce. Likewise dishes like paella and cheese based dished are all good companions for a dry rosé, cheese especially because of the saltiness.

Sweet foods - these make wine taste more bitter and astringent so if you start out with something dry it is going to seem thinner and acidic with sweet foods and it will tend to lose any fruitiness. The advice here is go for something at least as sweet as the food, so if it is a toffee banana may cause problem for any rose wine but a blush zinfandel will go nicely with moderately sweet foods. A surprising combination is to have an off dry German rosé with currywurst, sliced sausage in a sweet curry sauce, it works surprisingly well.

Eight watchwords for food and Wine pairings.
1. If you enjoy it then it's the right choice whatever any "rules" say
2. Avoid high acidity wines and cream sauces
3. High tannins are horrible with oily fish
4. Try to match the weight of the wine and the food so neither dominates
5. Sweet wines with fatty food – cheese, paté
6. Light zingy wines go well with acidic dishes with tomatoes and citrus
7. Tannic wines with red meat and game
8. Salmon and pink champagne

Rosé in (just over) a Page - The Do's And Don'ts

If you have absolutely no patience with this sort of thing and your significant other is making you read this then this page (and a bit) was written for you!

Choosing

First do try some rosé and don't dismiss it all because you have had a bad one – what would become of beer if we all did that!

- If you are a red drinker go for something made from a classic black grape like Syrah/Shiraz, Merlot or Cabernet Sauvignon.

- If you like a drier style then go for something from Provence in France or Navarra in Spain.

- If you like an off dry style go for a Rosé D'Anjou from the Loire valley in France

- If you like something a little sweeter and light go for a rosé Zinfandel – sometimes called blush or even white Zinfandel.

- For a party pink try a sparkling Cava from Penedes in Spain.

- Unless you are buying something very special which you know well always go for the current vintage – Rosé is about freshness and fruitiness not for storing in a dark cellar.

Serving

- Chill it, but not too much! Sweeter styles and sparkling can be well chilled but over chilling light wines will kill the fruitiness.

- Please never use coloured glasses – use a plastic cup if you have to but make it clear!

Enjoying it

You enjoy wine from the top of your head down:

- Look with the eyes – is it bright and clear
- Smell with the nose- is it clean, what can you smell, get the juices flowing,
- Taste with the mouth – take a good sip, swish it around, chew it enjoy it, swallow and appreciate
- Dance with the feet – mine are both of the left variety so I will leave this to your own judgement.

The Price of Wine

Apart from possibly a champagne or a rare bottle of celebrity produced wine, you are fairly unlikely to come across a rosé which is going to cause you to have to call your bank manager before making a purchase. Apart from the odd extravagant fizz all the wines in this book are under £15. Some actually were quite a bit less, but I implore you do not chase down the cheapest wine you can find and still expect to get something drinkable, at least not in the UK.

Let's just consider the cost of a bottle of wine, what goes into this product?

There is the agricultural element. Rents have to be paid on the land and the buildings, depreciation on tractors etc. Then there is the labour in the vineyard. Even with mechanised harvesting vines still need to be tended, pruned, checked for disease, sprayed. Also as anyone who has ever spoken to any sort of farmer will know they see life as a constant battle against the elements. In 2012 almost none of the quality English vineyards made any wine at all as the harvest was so bad after a terrible growing season.

Then there is the wine making. This requires considerable investment in the equipment, all of which has to be kept scrupulously clean. And then after you have spent all this money you store the wine, perhaps in oak barrels costing €800 a go for a couple of years.

Now finally you put the stuff in a bottle which means more equipment, labelling, and sealing with a cork or other modern device. You now load these into boxes and you have to ship them wherever they are going. You can save a bit on this by shipping the wine in a tanker or they even have containers kitted out with big plastic bags like an enormous wine box.

And when the wine finally arrives on our sceptered shores HMRC slap a great dollop of tax on it.

Now some of these costs can be finessed to keep them as low as possible but fundamentally you have to grow the grapes, make some wine, put it in a container, ship it somewhere and pay some tax.

Consider now the £4 bottle of wine. Most of that £4 is on packaging, shipping and tax. By some estimates the value of the actual wine in that bottle is around 29p. Yep, 29p. Now upgrade to a £5 bottle and because of the arcane way both taxation and commerce work you probably now have wine worth maybe 49p. That may not sound great but you now are drinking wine which cost nearly twice as much to make. Upgrade to the £10 a bottle shelf and you're getting wine which is starting to be a significant part of the price you paid and inconsequence is pretty much guaranteed to be a lot nicer.

Exact calculations vary somewhat but roughly speaking a representative table of costs would look something like this

Retail Price	£4.00	£5.00	£7.00	£10.00	£15.00	£25.00
Duty & VAT	2.61	2.81	3.21	3.81	4.81	6.81
Shipping	0.20	0.20	0.20	0.20	0.20	0.20
Retail Margin	1.90	1.50	2.10	3.00	4.50	7.50
Winemaking	0.29	0.49	1.49	2.99	5.49	10.49
As % of retail	0.25%	9.8%	21.3%	29.9%	36.6%	41.9%

Once you go down to £3.50 a bottle you are pretty much looking at 1p for the wine, and trust me that is not good value, just poor wine.

Lots of things make wine more expensive. Where the grapes are grown, what the grapes are it is made from, and specifically how well the vineyard is managed, which is a very labour intensive process. The harvesting is also a big factor, not simply man against machines but styles that call for late harvesting or the selection of bunches or even individual grapes means several passes through the vineyard. The ageing in oak, the cellaring for extended periods until it is ready to bottle all add to the costs. However, after this we start getting into marketing, branding, reputation and a whole other area which tends to double, quadruple, will generally up the price!

But how about those bargains with 50% off, or the exclusive wine clubs offering half price cases? Just ask yourself who set those retail prices to begin with. Sure there are rules that say a product has to be offered at that price for a period but that is easy enough to build into the business plan. In short caveat emptor, buyer beware.

My advice? Correct for inflation if you picked this book up at a car boot sale and stick in the £7.50 to £12 bracket for normal and keep it under £25 for special and you will seldom be disappointed unless you go out of your way to select a wine you actually hate.

Some Views from the Experts

I have spoken to a lot of people about rosé wine in the course of writing this book but here are a few comments from some particularly well informed wine enthusiasts - lawyers please note that is not a euphemism for "plonky"!

The Wine Masters

My internet discussions on Rosé wine attracted the eye of no less than three Masters of Wine. These are folk who have passed the notoriously difficult Master of Wine examinations. To gain the MW qualification candidates have to demonstrate a thorough knowledge of the global wine industry and an ability to taste and accurately evaluate wines blind. The Master of Wine is considered to be the peak professional qualification of the world's wine trade and has an international membership of approximately 300 – so 1% of them at least like the idea of this book! Find out more about them here www.mastersofwine.org.

Elizabeth Gabay MW

Elizabeth Gabay is a Master of Wine who writes on south east France, Hungary and northern Italy, notable credits include Oz Clarke Pocket Wine Guide (Provence and Corsica) and Jancis Robinson's 'World Atlas of Wine' (Provence). She recommends a couple of additional resources for discovering more about rosé wines:

- The rosé research centre in Vidauban (http://www.centredurose.fr/) for lots of technical information, training, etc
- Claude Flanzy's definitive book on Rosé wine - written in French - but he is THE expert.

She told me "I have done a lot of research on rosé myself for various conferences and articles and the question on whether there is more to defining the wine than just colour, is to me, the crux of the issue. I have judged at the Mondial du rosé and felt that in the end there was very little appreciation of the wide variety of rosé styles - some marked the wine down if it was too dark, some if there was too much residual sugar, too much fruit... I ended up being very frustrated as I wanted to learn about rosé as a style and felt I got nowhere.

Speak to winemakers in Provence and most will say it is the most difficult wine to make - to get the colour right with no tannin, to get enough fruit and enough acidity, neutral or a bigger wine to go with a meal."

Philip Goodband MW

Philip is an experienced WSET certified wine educator and is Senior Lecturer at the London International Wine and Spirit School. He is also Former Chairman of the Institute of Masters of Wine and chair of the Technical and Judging Committee of the IWSC.

He believes Rosé has some serious PR problems. He says "Even in wine competitions it is difficult to persuade judges to award gold medals for rose wines. Personally I believe there are many excellent Rosés in differing styles for differing occasions just as there are reds and whites.

Philip Reedman MW

Philip works in Australia as a wine consultant having been for many years Tesco's Senior Product Development manager.

Perhaps it is the Australian influence but Phil made a most refreshing remark for someone in the higher reaches of the world of wine – "....please, do cover White Zinfandel; perhaps the most despised category amongst industry snobs, but it is so important to so many consumers and a great gateway into wine." I trust he will be pleased to see it merits a detailed mention.

~~~~~~~~~~~~~~~~~~

Around the wider world of wine exporters, winemakers and retailers all joined in the debate. Here are a few of the comments they shared.

Cristiana Vitale

Cristina is a wine export manager from Venice, she says - "One of my clients, who, by the way has been the president of the Union International des Oenologues for 12 years, agrees rosé is more than just a picnic wine. He makes a classic method rosé and a and unique Moscato rosa (which is not a Moscato but is called so because an old cataloguing mistake) designed for the women. It is fresh, brilliant pink, with a delicate fragrance and a pleasing sweetness which makes a splendid after hours. It is the kind of wine which makes one to think sitting at a promenade in a cool evening"

Michael Cooper

Michael owns the Tomevinos wine store in Zaragoza. He waxed lyrical on Spanish Rosé - "In the Vinho Verde region you have Padeiro and Espadeiro grapes making excellent rosés, try Quinta Da Gomariz for example. In Spain I particularly enjoy some of the rosés from the Cigales region, Carredueñas has an interesting rosé that was barrel fermented. Also rosés made from the Mencia grape are delicious."

Óscar Quevedo

Oscar is the export manager for Quevedo Port Wine and perhaps understandably encouraged me to consider including a Rosé Port in the book which you will find in the Portugal section. He enthused about how a fresh, fruit and lovely young Port can taste and people will love to know about that. Let me know if you need tasting notes.

Nels Becker

Nels is the new National Sales Director at Bethel Heights Vineyards (interesting wine see USA section) having previously been at the Gruet Winery in Oregon. He is a real fan of the Pink Drink: "Whether it bubbles, dances with acidity, or blankets with a splash of RS, I enjoy the pink juice throughout the year. With so many regions and wines to choose from it's difficult to single out a specific location. We recently attended a Rosé dinner featuring 32 wines, Rosé from Piedmont, Tansmania, Bandol, Dundee, Yakima, Ribera del Duero, and surprisingly the stand out for balance and finish was AVV from Alexander Valley. Tasting is so subjective in the end, to the point, I highly suggest a glass of Rosé at least once a week throughout the year and it is an absolute blasphemy to go a month without a glass!" Now I am not going to argue with that!

Sources

I have gathered information from books conversations, magazines, and of course the internet. As far as possible the sources for these are listed her. My apologies to anyone who may inadvertently have been missed.

Books and Magazines

Wines and Spirits - Understanding style and quality WSET 2012

Wine and Grapes – Oz Clarke and Margaret Rand 2008

Wine Companion - – Hugh Johnson 1991

The Story of Wine – Hugh Johnson 1989

An Atlas of Wine – Hugh Johnson

Ben O'Donnell "The Cult of Wine 121 BC" – Wine Spectator March 2011

Vinexpo report 2013-09-01

Daniel Pambianchi – "10 Winemaking techniques you should know" WineMaker Jun 2008

Mike Potashnik PhD "Techniques for making Rosé Wine" – iWine review.com

Andrew Graham "Found- Australia's most interesting Rosé" – Australian Wine Review March 2012

Karien Lourens "Focus on Rosé" – WineLand January 2007

Susy Atkins – "Spanish rosado" – Daily Telegraph 25th May 2012

Eric Asimov "Rosés of a Different Color" New York Times July 5, 2011

Organisations

L'institut National De l'Origine et de la Qualité

Wines of Portugal

Conseil Interprofessionnel des Vins de Provence

Centre de Recherche et d'expérimentation sur le Vin Rosé

Vinos de España

Deutsches Weininstitut

The Wine and Spirit Trade Association

New Zealand Wine

Wines from Spain

Kobrand

Ministerio De Agricultura, Alimentación Y Medio Ambiente

Navarre Designation of Origin Regulatory Board

Web Sites

Appellationamerica.com

Alsace-wine.net

Blog.Bauduc.com – the blog of Angela and Gavin Quinney at Chateau Bauduc

Drvino.com

Diwinetaste.com

Justgoodwine.co.uk

Roserevolution.com

Sedimentality.com

spanishwine.com

Wine.appellationamerica.com

Winecountry.it

Wine-sa.com (Wines of South Africa)

wine-searcher.com

Yourlove of wine.com